Knit Three

Knit Three

ANGELA KING

GUILD PUBLISHING
LONDON

This edition published 1986 by
Book Club Associates by arrangement with
William Collins Sons & Co Ltd.

First published in Great Britain 1986
© Angela King 1986

British Library Cataloguing in Publication Data
King, Angela, *1950–*
Knit Three
1. Knitting-patterns
I. Title
646.4'304   TT820

Filmset in Souvenir by
Rowland Phototypesetting Ltd, Bury St Edmunds, Suffolk
Colour Reproduction by Dot Gradations Ltd, Chelmsford
Printed in Great Britain by
Wm Collins Sons & Co Ltd, London & Glasgow

Contents

ACKNOWLEDGEMENTS

The author and publishers gratefully acknowledge the help
of the following magazines, wool companies and
photographers who have given permission for their
photographs to be reproduced in this book. Photographs
were supplied courtesy of:

Living Magazine
Gingersnap, Florentine – photographer Ian Thomas
Violet, Sapphire, Peacock – photographer Roger Eaton
Double Cream, Double Cream Junior – photographer Sandra Lousada
Oyster, Voile – photographer Nick Briggs
Blue Moon – photographer Michael Woolley
Cowl, Rib, Big Cables, Squares – photographer Ian McKell

Woman's Own
Watercolour – photographer Rob Lee
Cobweb

Pins and Needles
Clashing Cables – photographer Henry Arden
Ninotchka

Over 21
Navy Lark – photographer Peter Ogilvy
Sideways Stretch – photographer Richard Dunkley
Le Rouge et le Noir – photographer Andy Lane
Long Shot

Good Housekeeping
Cool Neutral

Woman's Weekly
Farmer's Daughter

Woman
Abstract

Miz
Tailcoat and skirt – photographer Simon Bottomley
Fluorescent

Observer magazine
Tight Squeeze – photographer Robert Erdman

Pingouin leaflets
Geometric – leaflet no. 8446
Moss Rose – leaflet no. 8453
Short Cut – leaflet no. 8461

Gold Strike, Aztec – photographer Sandra Lousada
Golden Shot – photographer Dave J. Anthony

Most grateful thanks to the knitters who worked so hard to
make all the designs in this book:

Barbara Barrington	Mandy Goldman	Mary McDowell
May Begg	Dianne Howes	Fusako Ridley
Angela Chapman	Mary Hulatt	Harriet Sogbodjor
Rosalinde Goalen	Irene Igbenedion	Marjorie Vennall

Introduction

As the fashion element takes over more and more in knitting, it makes sense to think carefully about colour before you tackle a knitting project.

Yarn companies are now producing far more exciting colours in their ranges and not only the French yarn manufacturers, but also the more traditional British companies, are producing a really good choice of shades as well as textures. An afternoon spent just looking at the yarn on the shelves of a wool shop is time well spent, because it gives you an idea of what is available and how the different yarns look together.

For knitters who are keen on wondrously hued fair isles, the trend to more colour awareness has been led by artist and designer Kaffe Fassett, who makes brilliant use of colour in his work and encourages knitters to find their own colour combinations.

If you are keen to try fair isle knitting, developing your colour sense is vital, because although a design might look wonderful on the model, the colours used might not necessarily suit you. Using some of your left-over balls of yarn, try out colours against each other in quickly knitted stripes first of all, and compare them to the colours already in your wardrobe. When you have some shades that you like, knit up a sample of part of the design, repeating a simple fair isle motif in different shades, and you will then be able to decide which is best for you. Pinning up your sample on a board and looking at it from time to time will tell you if a colour stands out too brightly, so needing to be toned down, and if all the colours balance.

For those who claim to be hopeless with colour, a good initial guide is the method of picking two colours which make a beautiful contrast, such as red and navy. Now pick a colour which is a shade lighter or darker than one of these (or two extra colours which are lighter or darker), and add a neutral. It can be exciting to use clashing colours together, such as red and orange, or shocking pink, red and violet, toned down with black and beige, or steel grey.

If you dislike wearing multi-coloured garments, you can still make unexpected colour contrasts in the way you put your outfit together, using the same method of checking the colour of the knitted sample against your wardrobe before you begin to knit, teaming turquoise, say, with khaki, scarlet with violet or peach with taupe. Even if you always wear classic colours you will be amazed how many different shades of cream there are.

If you want to develop your colour sense, there are many ways you can get ideas. The cinema is a good source of inspiration, both of colour and shape. Art galleries are the obvious place to visit to look at beautiful colours, and fashion magazines are helpful. You'll get a lot of inspiration from country walks, as you study wild flowers, or examine shells and pebbles on a beach.

Discovering an unusual colour combination which perfectly suits you is really exciting because, after all, if you are going to the trouble of knitting a sweater, you want to be sure before you start that it is going to look good.

How to Knit

Casting on

The thumb method (using only one needle) Leave a piece of yarn hanging down which is long enough to form the number of stitches required. Make a slip loop and put it on to the needle. Hold the loose end of yarn in your left hand and make a loop on your left thumb (a). Insert the needle into the loop (b), wrap the yarn round the needle (c) and draw it through the loop on the thumb (d) as you slip the loop from the thumb and gently tighten the left-hand thread (e). You have now formed the first stitch. Repeat the process for the rest of the row.

The two-needle method Make a slip loop and place it on the left-hand needle. Insert the right-hand needle into it, wind the yarn round the right-hand needle, draw a loop through and place this loop on to the left-hand needle. Continue in this way, working into the last stitch on the left-hand needle each time.

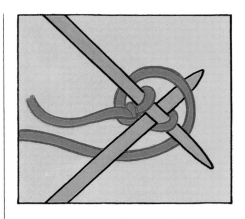

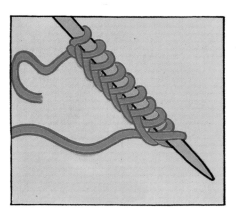

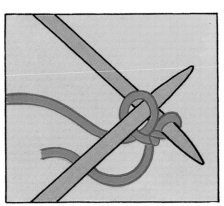

Casting on

Casting off

Knit the first two stitches of the row. With the point of the left-hand needle, lift the stitch furthest to the right on the right-hand needle over the stitch next to it, leaving one stitch on the right-hand needle. Knit one more stitch, making

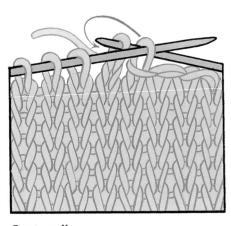

Casting off

two stitches on the right-hand needle. Lift the one furthest to the right over the other, as before. Continue in this way until only one stitch of the row remains. Cut the yarn and pass it through this stitch to fasten off.

How to knit a stitch

Hold the needle with the cast-on stitches in the left hand. With the yarn at the back of the work, insert the right-hand needle into the front of the first loop on the left-hand needle, front to back, left to right. Wind the yarn round the point of the right-hand needle and draw a loop through the loop on the left-hand needle, while slipping this left-hand stitch. The new stitch is now on the right-hand needle. Continue in this way until there are no more stitches on the left-hand needle. Transfer the right-hand needle to the left hand and begin the second row.

How to knit a stitch

How to purl a stitch

Hold the needle with the cast-on stitches in the left hand. With the yarn at the front of the work, insert the right-hand needle into the front of the first stitch, back to front, right to left. Take the yarn round the point of the right-hand needle over the top and under, from right to left. Draw this loop through the stitch on the left-hand needle, while slipping the left-hand stitch. The new stitch is now on the right-hand needle. Continue in this way until there are no more stitches on the left-hand needle, then start a new row.

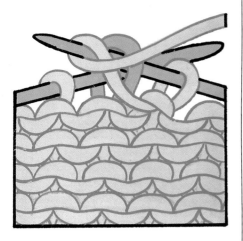

How to purl a stitch

How to increase

There are different ways of making extra stitches, some of which make holes: these are used in lace knitting when the hole is part of the lacy pattern.

Invisible increasing This is usually used to shape side edges. Insert the right-hand needle into the next stitch on the left-hand needle and knit into it, but do not slip the original stitch off the left-hand needle; now knit into the *back* of this stitch, making two stitches. The abbreviation for this method is usually 'inc. 1 st.'

How to decrease

If you are working a knit row, insert the right-hand needle knitwise into the second stitch and then into the first stitch on the left-hand needle and knit them together.

If working a purl row, insert the needle into the first stitch then the second stitch on the left-hand needle and purl them together.

Checking your tension

Tension means how tightly or how loosely your knitting is worked. Dull though it may be, it is vitally important to check your tension or your garment will not come out the right size. If you hate knitting a tension square, check your actual work by measuring the number of rows and stitches to the number of centimetres or inches quoted at the top of the pattern. If you have fewer stitches, change your needles to a size *smaller*. If you have more stitches, change your needles to a size *larger*. If you are making up your own design instructions, of

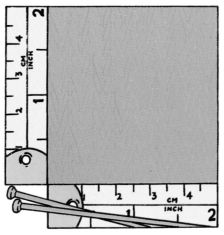

Tension

course, you can work to any tension you wish to.

Abbreviations

Many beginner knitters complain they cannot understand knitting patterns. This is because they have skipped the information at the beginning of the pattern, where the abbreviations are listed. Abbreviations can be confusing because they are not standardised, so different designers may use the same ones and mean completely different things, although the basic ones are always the same. However, once you have read them through, you should be able to understand what the pattern means. Abbreviations are necessary because they save space, and once you have learnt what they mean it is really easy to find your way through any pattern.

Reading ball bands

If you have a look at the ball band round your ball of yarn, you will find that it contains a surprising amount of helpful information. Many ball bands give a suggested needle size and sometimes a suggested tension, too. If you want to design your own patterns, this information is really useful. In addition, you will find symbols giving help on washing, pressing, and dry cleaning.

Joining in yarn

It is always better to do this by joining the yarn in at the beginning or end of a row. Although this leaves long ends, you can use them for sewing up afterwards. If you join in the middle of a row, sooner or later the join may give and become a hole, however well you have grafted it, and knotted yarn in the middle of a row looks really ghastly.

Pressing

Pressing makes a terrific difference to the look of the finished garment, so it is definitely worth the bother. Not all knitting needs to be pressed – check the instructions on the ball band. If you press too hard, you could ruin your careful handiwork by flattening the stitches beyond repair – yarn is fragile, after all, so take it gently.

To press, pin out each piece to the measurement given in the pattern, with the wrong side of the work uppermost. Using a damp, dry or wet cloth (check ball band to find out which) and a warm iron, begin to press by raising and lowering the iron. NEVER move the iron back and forth as in ordinary ironing, or you will ruin the yarn. If pressing cotton, you can be a bit firmer. The pattern will tell you which parts of the garment need to be pressed.

Sewing up

Even if you have knitted all the pieces beautifully, bad sewing up will make a mess of your work. Proper sewing up is really easy once you have the knack.

Invisible seaming An invisible seam is best for side and sleeve seams. You are going to sew two pieces together so that you won't be able to see there is a join. The trick is to sew with the RIGHT side of the pieces uppermost. Place the two edges of each piece close together. Begin by securing the yarn at one end and bring the needle and yarn to the right side of the work. Bring the needle across and insert it under the thread that connects the first and second stitch of the row. Draw the needle and yarn through then insert them through the same thread of the other piece of knitting. Continue to weave across the two pieces in this way, drawing them together firmly but not tightly.

Back stitch seaming Use a back stitch seam when the seam runs across the grain of the knitting, as in the shoulder seam, or along a shaped edge. Place the two edges together with the right sides inside and fasten the yarn at the right-hand edge at the back of the work. Work the seam from right to left, moving one stitch to the right at the front and two to the left at the back of the work.

Knitting with colours

Knitting with colours, called fair isle knitting, offers wonderful creative possibilities and hours of pleasure in the actual technique. However, you have to spend a bit of time mastering the method when you start. The main problem with fair isle is what to do with the colours at the back of the work. If you know what you are doing, the back of your knitting will be as neat as the front. If you are not doing it properly, an awful snarl of colours will be tangled at the back and the front will be full of gaping holes, so the time taken to learn fair isle properly really is worth it.

Some fair isle patterns are in word form, but most are worked from a chart, so study this first.

Reading a chart Each *symbol* in the chart represents a colour. To find out which colour, look at the *key*. Each square of the chart refers to one stitch and one row. The chart gives you one *repeat* of the pattern. The number of stitches in the repeat should divide into the number of stitches in your row – although there may be a *selvedge stitch* at each end of every row (selvedge stitches are used for sewing up). The numbers printed at the sides of the chart are the *rows* which make up the pattern repeat.

Fair isle is nearly always worked in *stocking stitch*. Therefore all *odd-numbered* rows on the chart are *knit* rows and all *even numbered* rows are *purl* rows. Knit rows are worked from right to left on the chart and purl rows are worked from left to right.

Dealing with the yarns at the back Once you have mastered this section, you can prevent your yarns from getting into a tangle.

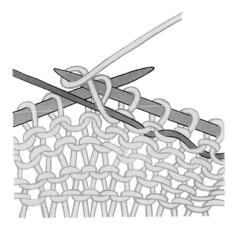

Weaving

Weaving The colours not in use are carried over the yarn in use for one stitch, weaving in one strand at a time, and under the yarn in use for the next stitch, on the wrong side of the work. This makes the fabric rather stiff and solid, so the method is best for socks and gloves.

Stranding If the different colours are spaced only four or five stitches apart, strand the yarn not in use by carrying it across the back of the work. *Twist* the yarns concerned when changing colours to avoid holes.

If different colours are spaced very widely apart, you can still use the stranding method, but this time catch the colour not in use by dropping it over the colour in use at every four or five stitches.

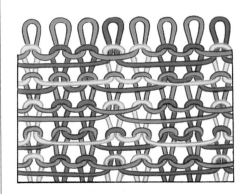

Stranding

When very large areas of one colour are part of a design, it is best not to strand or weave, but to use different balls of yarn for each area, remembering to twist to avoid holes.

When either weaving or stranding, remember to do both *loosely* or your work will pucker badly. (This is one of the easiest mistakes to make in fair isle.) To avoid puckering, gently spread out the last eight or ten stitches on the right-hand needle so that your work is slightly stretched. Now take up the next colour and continue knitting. Try to keep the back of your work as tidy as you can. For an even finish, one colour should always be kept above and the other beneath.

Knitting in the ends You will save a lot of boring darning in at the sewing up stage if you do this. When you have finished with a colour, knit it in by dropping it over the yarn in use. Knit a stitch and repeat this three or four times before cutting the yarn of the colour no longer in use.

Dealing with tangles Try not to let the yarns get too badly tangled at the back – you'll save a lot of time this way. Methods of keeping the colours separate are:
1 keep the colours in small balls and loop a slip knot or elastic band over each to prevent them unwinding.
2 use special bobbins.

Finally, when attempting your first fair isle, do knit a stitch sample. You will save yourself so much time and effort if you check your tension first and practise the pattern before you begin to knit the actual garment.

Knitting with a circular needle
The modern 'funnel' collar is best worked on a circular needle, without a seam. Many knitters refuse to try these needles, but they are in fact very easy to use. Circular needles are made of flexible plastic with knitting needles at each end, and can be bought in varying lengths. If you buy one too long for the purpose you intend, it will stretch the work out of shape, so aim to buy one which will enable the stitches to reach

the needle points at each end without stretching the knitting beyond the correct tension. It is also fine to use a needle which is shorter than this – as long as the stitches are not uncomfortably crowded.

USEFUL INFORMATION

Needle Conversions

UK and Australian metric	UK and Australian original, Canada, S. Africa	USA
2mm.	14	00
2¼mm.	13	0
2¾mm.	12	1
3mm.	11	2
3¼mm.	10	3
3¾mm.	9	4
4mm.	8	5
4½mm.	7	6
5mm.	6	7
5½mm.	5	8
6mm.	4	9
6½mm.	3	10
7mm.	2	10½
7½mm.	1	11
8mm.	0	12
9mm.	00	13
10mm.	000	15

American Terminology
Most knitting terms are identical in English and American usage. The exceptions to this are listed below, with the English term used in the book given first, followed by the American term.

Stocking stitch (st. st.) = stockinette stitch (st. st.); yarn round needle (y.r.n.) = yarn over needle (y.o.n.), cast off = bind off; tension = gauge.

Metric Conversion Tables

Length (to the nearest ¼in.)				Weight (rounded up to the nearest ¼oz.)	
cm.	in.	cm.	in.	g.	oz.
1	½	55	21¾	25	1
2	¾	60	23½	50	2
3	1¼	65	25½	100	3¾
4	1½	70	27½	150	5½
5	2	75	29½	200	7¼
6	2½	80	31½	250	9
7	2¾	85	33½	300	10¾
8	3	90	35½	350	12½
9	3½	95	37½	400	14¼
10	4	100	39½	450	16
11	4¼	110	43½	500	17¾
12	4¾	120	47	550	19½
13	5	130	51¼	600	21¼
14	5½	140	55	650	23
15	6	150	59	700	24¾
16	6¼	160	63	750	26½
17	6¾	170	67	800	28¼
18	7	180	70¾	850	30
19	7½	190	74¾	900	31¾
20	8	200	78¾	950	33¾
25	9¾	210	82¾	1000	35½
30	11¾	220	86½	1200	42¼
35	13¾	230	90½	1400	49¼
40	15¾	240	94½	1600	56½
45	17¾	250	98½	1800	63½
50	19¾	300	118	2000	70½

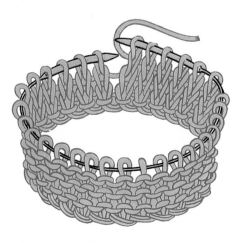

Circular needle

The Patterns

Cobweb

MATERIALS

6 50 g. balls Pingouin Mohair 70 or 18 25g. balls W. H. Smith Brushed Mohair; a pair each 5 mm. (no. 6) and 6 mm. (no. 4) long knitting needles; 6 buttons.

TENSION

16 stitches and 24 rows to 10 cm. (4 in.) square using 6 mm. (no. 4) needles.

MEASUREMENTS

To fit bust 81–97 cm., 32–38 in.
Length 64 cm., 25 in.
Cuff to cuff 127 cm., 50 in.

ABBREVIATIONS

alt., alternate; beg., beginning; cont., continue; dec., decreas(e)ing; foll., following; inc., increas(e)ing; k., knit; p., purl; patt., pattern; p.s.s.o., pass slip stitch over; rem., remain(ing); rep., repeat; sl., slip; sts., stitches; st. st., stocking stitch; tog., together; y.f., yarn forward.

INSTRUCTIONS

Beg. at left cuff edge. With 5 mm. needles, cast on 45 sts. Work 20 rows k. 1, p. 1 rib, beg. alt. rows p. 1.
Next row: K. 1, * (k. 1, p. 1, k. 1) in next st.; rep. from * to last st., k. 1 – 131 sts. Change to 6 mm. needles and cont. in patt. thus:
* Row 1 (right side): K. 1, (y.f., k. 3, sl. 1, k. 2 tog., p.s.s.o., k. 3, y.f., k. 1) to end.

If you love lace knitting, this fine mohair batwing jacket will give you lots of pleasure to make.

Row 2 and every foll. alt. row: K.
Row 3: K. 1, (k. 1, y.f., k. 2, sl. 1, k. 2 tog., p.s.s.o., k. 2, y.f., k. 2) to end.
Row 5: K. 1, (k. 2, y.f., k. 1, sl. 1, k. 2 tog., p.s.s.o., k. 1, y.f., k. 3) to end.
Row 7: K. 1, (k. 3, y.f., sl. 1, k. 2 tog., p.s.s.o., y.f., k. 4) to end.
Row 8: K.
These 8 rows form the patt. Rep. them once more. *

To shape sides Keeping patt. correct, cast on 2 sts. at beg. of next 2 rows. Inc. 1 st. at both ends of next row and foll. 2 alt. rows, ending after wrong-side row. Rep. last 8 rows 4 times more – 181 sts. Patt. 48 rows straight.

To shape neck Next row: Patt. 91 sts., turn; leave rem. sts. on spare needle. Patt. 38 rows more on these sts. for back, thus ending after 7th patt. row. Leave sts. on spare needle. With right side facing, join yarn at neck edge to rem. sts. and cont. for left front thus: cast off 4 sts. at beg. of next row, and 3 sts. at beg. of foll. 7 alt. rows. Cast off rem. 65 sts.
Cont. for right front thus: with 6 mm. needles, cast on 65 sts. and k. 1 row.
Row 1: Cast on 3 and k. these 3 sts., (y.f., k. 3, sl. 1, k. 2 tog., p.s.s.o., k. 3, y.f., k. 1) to last 5 sts., y.f., k. 3, k. 2 tog. Cont. in patt., casting on 3 sts. at beg. of foll. 6 alt.

rows and 4 sts. at beg. of 7th alt. row – 90 sts.
Next row: K. 90, then k. across sts. from back – 181 sts. Patt. 48 rows straight.

To shape sides Dec. 1 st. at both ends of next row and foll. 2 alt. rows, ending after wrong-side row. Cast off 2 sts. at beg. of next 2 rows. Rep. last 8 rows 4 times more – 131 sts. Work from * to *. Change to 5 mm. needles.
Next row: K. 1, (sl. 1, k. 2 tog., p.s.s.o.) to last st., k. 1 – 45 sts. Rib 20 rows as left cuff. Cast off in rib.

Bottom band

Join side and underarm seams. With right side facing, using 5 mm. needles, pick up and k. 58 sts. along left bottom edge, 94 sts. from back, 58 sts. along right bottom edge – 210 sts.
Next row: (K. 1, p. 2 tog.) to end – 140 sts. Work 20 rows k. 1, p. 1 rib. Cast off in rib.

Front band

With right side, facing, using 5 mm. needles, pick up and k. 90 sts. up right front edge to neck shaping, 40 sts. up neck edge, 48 sts. along back neck, 40 sts. down neck edge, 90 sts. to base of left front – 308 sts.
Work 3 rows k. 1, p. 1 rib.
Next row: (buttonholes) Rib 4, (cast off 2, rib 15, including st. on needle after cast off) 5 times, cast off 2, rib to end. Rib 6 rows more casting on 2 sts. over those cast off on 1st row. Cast off in rib.

TO MAKE UP

Do not press. Sew on buttons.

Farmer's Daughter

Cosy Aran sweater in a bobble and honeycomb cable pattern with double moss stitch is quick to knit because of the thick yarn.

MATERIALS

13 (14, 14, 15, 15) 50 g. balls Hayfield Grampian Chunky or 17 (18, 18, 19, 19) 50 g. balls of W. H. Smith Pure Wool Chunky; a pair each 6 mm. (no. 4) and 5½ mm. (no. 5) knitting needles; a cable needle.

TENSION

14 stitches and 20 rows to 10 cm. (4 in.) over double moss stitch using 6 mm. (no. 4) needles; 1 cable panel measures 11 cm. (4½ in.) using 6 mm. (no. 4) needles.

MEASUREMENTS

To fit bust 81 (86, 91, 97, 102) cm., 32 (34, 36, 38, 40) in.
All round at underarms 85.5 (91, 97, 102.5, 108) cm., 33½ (36, 38, 40¼, 42½) in.
Side seam (all sizes) 37 cm., 14½ in.
Length 53 (55, 57, 59, 61) cm., 20¾ (21½, 22½, 23¼, 24) in.
Sleeve seam (all sizes) 43 cm., 17 in.

ABBREVIATIONS

c. 4b., cable 4 back (slip next 2 sts. on to cable needle and leave at back of work, k. 2, then k. 2, from cable needle); c. 4f., cable 4 front (as c. 4b., but leave sts. at front of work); dec., decrease (by working 2 sts. tog.); d. m. st., double moss st.; inc., increase (by working twice into same st.); k., knit plain; m.b., make bobble (k. 1, p. 1, k. 1, p. 1, all into same st., turn, p. 4, turn, k. 4, then pass the 2nd, 3rd and 4th sts. over 1st st.); nil, means nothing is worked here for this size; p., purl; s.r., single rib (k. 1 and p. 1 alternately); st., stitch; tog., together.

INSTRUCTIONS

Back

With 5½ mm. needles cast on 57 (61, 65, 69, 73) sts. and beginning odd-numbered rows with p. 1 and even-numbered rows with k. 1 work 13 rows in single rib.
Next (inc.) row: Rib 7 (9, 11, 2, 4), * inc., rib 1 (1, 1, 2, 2); repeat from * until 6 (8, 10, 1, 3) st(s). remain(s), rib to end – 79 (83, 87, 91, 95) sts.
Change to 6 mm. needles and work the 8-row pattern as follows:
Row 1: * P. 1, k. 1 *; work from * to * 3 (4, 5, 6, 6) times, ** p. 2, k. 8, p. 2, m.b. p. 2, k. 8, p. 2 **; k. 1, work from * to * 6 (6, 6, 6, 8) times, work from ** to ** once, then * k. 1, p. 1; work from this * 3, (4, 5, 6, 6) times.
Row 2: * K. 1, p. 1 *; work from * to * 3 (4, 5, 6, 6) times, ** k. 2, p. 8, k. 2, p. 1, k. 2, p. 8, k. 2 **; p. 1, work from * to * 6 (6, 6, 6, 8) times, work from ** to ** once, then * p. 1, k. 1; work from this * 3 (4, 5, 6, 6) times.
Row 3: * K. 1, p. 1 *; work from * to * 3 (4, 5, 6, 6) times, ** p. 2, c. 4b., c. 4f., p. 2, k. 1, p. 2, c. 4b., c. 4f., p. 2 **; p. 1, work from * to * 6 (6, 6, 6, 8) times, work from ** to ** once, then * p. 1, k. 1; work from this * 3 (4, 5, 6, 6) times.
Row 4: * P. 1, k. 1 *; work from * to * 3 (4, 5, 6, 6) times, ** k. 2, p. 8, k. 2, p. 1, k. 2, p. 8, k. 2 **; k. 1, work from * to * 6 (6, 6, 6, 8) times, work from ** to ** once, then * k. 1, p. 1; work from this * 3 (4, 5, 6, 6) times.
These 4 rows form the pattern for the d. m. st. panels at each end and at centre.
Row 5: As row 1.
Row 6: As row 2.
Row 7: D. m. st. 8 (10, 12, 14, 14), * p. 2, c. 4f., c. 4b., p. 2, k. 1, p. 2, c. 4f., c. 4b., p. 2 *; d. m. st. 13 (13, 13, 13, 17), work from * to * once, d. m. st. 8 (10, 12, 14, 14).
Row 8: As row 4.
Pattern a further 52 rows.

To shape raglan armholes Keeping

17

continuity of pattern, cast off 4 sts. at the beginning of each of the next 2 rows ***, then dec. 1 st. at each end of the next row and the 14 (16, 18, 20, 22) following alternate rows – 41 sts.
For the 81 (86, 91, 97) cm. (32 (34, 36, 38) in.) sizes only:
Next row: Pattern 4, * p. 2 tog. *; work from * to * 3 (3, 3, 2) times, pattern 17 (17, 17, 21), work from * to * 4 (4, 4, 3) times, pattern 4 – 33 (33, 33, 35) sts.
For the 102 cm. (40 in.) size only:
Next row: Pattern 2, * p. 2 tog., pattern 4, p. 2 tog. *; pattern 21, work from * to * once, pattern 2 – 37 sts.
For all sizes: Leave these sts. on a spare needle.

Front
Work as given for back to ***, then dec. 1 st. at each end of the next row and the 10 (12, 14, 16, 18) following alternate rows – 49 sts.

To divide for neck *Next row:* Pattern 12, work 3 tog. and leave these 13 sts. on a spare needle for right half neck, pattern 19 and leave these sts. on a st. holder, work 3 tog., pattern 12 and work on these 13 sts. for left half neck.
The left half neck: Dec. 1 st. at neck edge on each of the next 7 rows, at the same time dec. 1 st. at armhole edge on the 1st of these rows and the 3 following alternate rows – 2 sts. Work 1 row, then k. 2 tog. and fasten off.
The right half neck: With right side of work facing, rejoin yarn to inner end of the 13 sts. left on spare needle and work as given for left half neck.

Sleeves (both alike)
With 5½ mm. needles cast on 37 (39, 39, 43, 47) sts. and, beginning with a 2nd rib row, work 13 rows in rib as given on back.
Next (inc.) row: Rib 1 (2, 2, 4, 6), * inc., rib 1; repeat from * until nil (1, 1, 3, 5) st(s). remain(s), rib to end – 55 (57, 57, 61, 65) sts.
Change to 6 mm. needles and work in pattern as follows:
Row 1: K. 1 (nil, nil, nil, nil), * p. 1, k. 1; work from * 4 (5, 5, 6, 7) times, p. 2, k. 8, p. 2, m.b., p. 3, m. b., p. 3, m. b., p. 2, k. 8, p. 2, * k. 1, p. 1; work from this * 4 (5, 5, 6, 7) times, k. 1 (nil, nil, nil, nil).
Row 2: P. 1 (nil, nil, nil, nil), * k. 1, p. 1; work from * 4 (5, 5, 6, 7) times, k. 2, p. 8, k. 2, p. 1, k. 3, p. 1, k. 3, p. 1, k. 2, p. 8, k. 2, * p. 1, k. 1; work from this * 4 (5, 5, 6, 7) times, p. 1 (nil, nil, nil, nil).
Row 3: P. 1 (nil, nil, nil, nil), * k. 1, p. 1; work from * 4 (5, 5, 6, 7) times, p. 2, c. 4b., c. 4f., p. 2, k. 1, p. 3, k. 1, p. 3, k. 1, p. 2, c. 4b., c. 4f., p. 2, * p. 1, k. 1; work from this * 4 (5, 5, 6, 7) times, p. 1 (nil, nil, nil, nil).
Row 4: K. 1 (nil, nil, nil, nil), * p. 1, k. 1; work from * 4 (5, 5, 6, 7) times, k. 2, p. 8, k. 2, p. 1, k. 3, p. 1, k. 3, p. 1, k. 2, p. 8, k. 2, * k. 1, p. 1; work from this * 4 (5, 5, 6, 7) times, k. 1 (nil, nil, nil, nil).
These 4 rows form the pattern for the d. m. st. panels at each end and bobble panel at centre.
Keeping continuity of pattern as set, working cables to match back, pattern a further 68 rows.

To shape raglan sleeve top Keeping continuity of pattern, cast off 4 sts. at the beginning at each of the next 2 rows, then dec. 1 st. at each end of the next 7 (5, nil, nil, nil) rows. Work 1 (1, nil, nil, nil) row, then dec. 1 st. at each end of the next row and the 10 (13, 18, 20, 22) following alternate rows – 11 sts.
Work 1 row, then leave these sts. on a safety pin.

Neckband
First join right raglan seams, then left sleeve to front only. With right side of work facing, using 5½ mm. needles, k. across the 11 sts. of left sleeve, pick up and k. 6 sts. down the left side of neck, k. across the 19 sts. at centre front decreasing 2 sts. evenly across these sts., pick up and k. 6 sts. up right side of neck, k. across the 11 sts. of right sleeve, and finally, k. across the 33 (33, 33, 35, 37) sts. at back neck, decreasing (increasing, increasing, increasing, increasing) 1 st. at the centre of these sts. – 83 (85, 85, 87, 89) sts. Beginning with the 2nd rib row as given on back, work 12 rows in single rib.
Cast off loosely in rib.

TO MAKE UP
Do not press. Join remaining raglan seam, continuing seam across neckband. Join side and sleeve seams. Fold neckband in half to wrong side and slip st. into position.

Golden Shot

Easy-fitting fair isle cardigan looks good in striking yellow and navy with jeans.

MATERIALS

6 (7) 50 g. balls Hayfield Grampian Double Knit in main colour, 2 (2) 50 g. balls 1st contrast colour and 3 (3) 50 g. balls 2nd contrast colour; a pair each 3¾ mm. (no. 9) and 4 mm. (no. 8) knitting needles; 3 buttons; spare needles; stitch holders.

Note For best results, use *only* recommended yarn.

TENSION

1 repeat of the pattern (12 stitches) measures 5 cm. (2 in.) in width, using 4 mm. (no. 8) needles.

MEASUREMENTS

To fit bust 82–86 (92–97) cm., 32–34 (36–38) in. very loosely.
Actual all round measurement 112 (122) cm., 44 (49) in.
Length 63.5 (65) cm., 25 (25½) in.
Sleeve seam (all sizes) approx. 46 cm., 18 in.

ABBREVIATIONS

beg., beginning; con., continue; dec., decrease; foll., following; inc., increase; k., knit; M., main colour; p., purl; patt., pattern; rem., remain(ing); rep., repeat; RS, right side; st(s)., stitch(es); st. st., stocking stitch; WS, wrong side.

INSTRUCTIONS

Back

Using 3¾ mm. needles and M., cast on 118 (130) sts. and work 6 cm. (2½ in.) in k. 1, p. 1 rib.
Inc. row: Rib 9 (9), * inc. 1, rib 6 (7), rep. from * 13 times more, inc. 1, rib 10 (8) – 133 (145) sts.
Change to 4 mm. needles.
Work in st. st. beg. with a k. row and patt. from chart, joining in and breaking off yarns when necessary, twisting yarns

when changing colour to avoid a gap; read RS rows from right to left and p. rows from left to right, working the 12 st. rep. 11 (12) times across row and edge st. as indicated.
Cont. straight in patt. until back measures 41 cm. (16 in.) from cast-on edge, ending with a wrong side row.

To shape for square armholes Cast off 18 (24) sts. at beg. of next 2 rows – 97 sts. both sizes.
Cont. straight in patt. until work measures 63.5 (65) cm. (25 (25½) in.) from cast-on edge, ending with a WS row.

To shape shoulders Cast off 26 sts. at beg. of next 2 rows. Cast off rem. 45 sts. for back neck edge.

Pocket linings (make 2)

Using 4 mm. needles and M., cast on 29 sts. and, starting with a k. row, work 14 cm. (5½ in.) in st. st., ending with a WS row. Leave sts. on a spare needle.

Left front

Using 3¾ mm. needles and M., cast on 64 (70) sts. and work 6 cm. (2¼ in.) in k. 1, p. 1 rib inc. 1 st. at both ends of last row and 1 st. in centre on 2nd size only –

66 (73) sts.
Change to 4 mm. needles.
1st size only Work in patt. from chart, thus working the 12-st. rep. 5 times across and with 6 sts. at front edge as shown.
2nd size only Work in patt. as on back thus working the 12-st. rep. 6 times with 1 edge st. as shown.
Both sizes Cont. straight in patt. until work measures 24 cm. (8½ in.) from cast-on edge, ending with a WS row.

Pocket row Patt. 10, slip next 29 sts. on to a stitch-holder and in their place patt. across sts. of one pocket back, then patt. 27 (34).
Work 1 row straight in patt.

To shape front neck Keeping patt. correct, dec. 1 st. at end (front edge) on next and every foll. 4th row until work measures same as back to armholes, ending at side edge.

To shape armhole and cont. neck shaping Cast off 18 (24) sts. at beg. of next row. Keeping armhole edge straight cont. to dec. 1 st. at front edge on every 4th row as set until 26 sts. rem. Cont. straight in patt. until work measures same as back to shoulders, ending with a WS row.
Cast off straight across for shoulder.

Right front

Work as given for left front reversing all shapings and pocket row on both sizes, also position of patt. on 1st size.

Sleeves (both alike)

Using 3¾ mm. needles and M., cast on

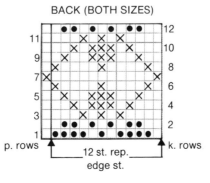

BACK (BOTH SIZES)

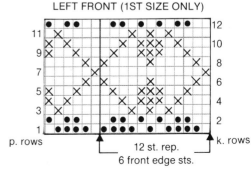

LEFT FRONT (1ST SIZE ONLY)

KEY   □ main shade   • 1st contrast   ✕ 2nd contrast

52 sts. and work 6 cm. (2¼ in.) in k. 1, p. 1 rib.

Inc. row: Rib 5, * inc. 1, rib. 4, rep. from * 7 times more, inc. 1, rib 6 – 61 sts. Change to 4 mm. needles.

Work 2 rows straight in patt. as on back. Keeping patt. correct and working extra sts. into the patt. as they occur, inc. 1 st. at both ends of next and every foll. 4th row until there are 81 sts. then on every 4th (3rd) row until there are 97 (109) sts. on the needle.

Cont. straight until sleeve seam measures approx. 46 cm. (18¼ in.) from cast-on edge, ending with a WS row and same patt. row as back/front to armhole shaping.

Place a marker at both ends of last row. Work a further 7.5 (10) cm. (3 (4) in.) straight in patt.

Cast off loosely straight across.

Pocket edgings (both alike)

Slip 29 sts. of one pocket top on to a 3¾ mm. needle, rejoin M. on right side.

Beg. and ending RS rows with p. 1 and WS rows with k. 1, work 8 rows in k. 1, p. 1 rib.

Cast off fairly loosely in rib.

Front band

Using 3¾ mm. needles and M., cast on 12 sts. and work 6 rows in k. 1, p. 1 rib.

1st buttonhole row Rib 5, cast off 2 sts., rib to end.

2nd buttonhole row Rib casting on 2 sts. over those cast off.

Cont. in rib working a further 2 buttonholes spaced 9 cm. (3½ in.) apart, then cont. straight until band, when slightly stretched, is long enough to be sewn up right front, round neck edge and down left front. Cast off in rib.

TO MAKE UP

Press st.st. parts as instructed on ball band. Sew pocket backs into position on WS and row ends of pocket tops to RS. Join shoulder seams. Set in sleeves, sewing the row ends above markers to the sts. cast off for armholes on both back and front and cast off edge to straight row ends on armholes. Join side and sleeve seams. Neatly sew band into position. Sew on buttons.

Short Cut

MATERIALS

7 (8, 8) 50 g. balls Pingouin Givre, or 6
(7, 8) 50 g. balls Pingouin Orage; a pair
each 5½ mm. (no. 5) and 6 mm. (no. 4)
knitting needles; cable needle.

TENSION

14 stitches and 17 rows to 10 cm. (4 in.)
using 6 mm. (no. 4) needles and stocking stitch.

MEASUREMENTS

To fit bust 86 (91, 97) cm., 34 (36, 38) in.
Length 42 (43, 44) cm., 16½ (17, 17½)
in.
Sleeve seam (all sizes) 46 cm., 18 in.

ABBREVIATIONS

C6L, slip next 2 sts. on to cable needle
and leave at front of work, k. 2, p. 2 then
k. 2 from cable needle; C6R, slip next 4
sts. on to cable needle and leave at back
of work, k. 2, then p. 2 and k. 2 from
cable needle; dec., decrease; foll., following; k., knit; inc., increase; p., purl;
patt., pattern; rep., repeat; st(s)., stitch-
(es); tog., together.

INSTRUCTIONS

SHORT VERSION

Back
Using 5½ mm. needles, cast on 87 (91,
95) sts. and work in k. 1, p. 1 rib for 7
rows, inc. 1 st. at end of last rib row – 88
(92, 96) sts.

Change to 6 mm. needles and work in
patt. as folls.
Row 1: K. 35 (37, 39), p. 3, k. 2, p. 2, k.
4, p. 2, k. 2, p. 3, k. 35 (37, 39).
Row 2: P. 35 (37, 39), k. 3, p. 2, k. 2, p.
4, k. 2, p. 2, k. 3, p. 35 (37, 39).
Rows 3 to 6: As Rows 1 and 2, twice.
Row 7: K. 35 (37, 39), p. 3, C6R, C6L, p.
3, k. 35 (37, 39).
Rows 8 to 11: As Rows 1 and 2, twice.
Rows 12 to 16: K.
These 16 rows form patt. ** Cont in patt.
until work measures 38 (39, 40) cm., (15
(15½, 15¾) in.), ending with a wrong
side row.

To shape neck K. 29 (31, 33), k. 2 tog.,
turn.
Dec. 1 st. at neck edge on the next 3
rows. 27 (29, 31) sts. Cast off. Slip centre
26 sts. on to a spare needle, rejoin yarn
to remaining sts. and complete to match
first side, reversing shapings.

Front
Work as for back to **.
Cont. in patt. until work measures 35
(36, 37) cm. (13¾ (14, 14¾) in.), ending
with a wrong side row.

To shape neck K. 33 (35, 37), k. 2 tog.,
turn.
Dec. 1 st. at next edge on every row to
27 (29, 31) sts. Cont. straight until front
matches back to shoulders. Cast off. Slip
centre 18 sts. on to a spare needle.
Rejoin yarn to remaining sts. and complete to match first side, reversing shapings.

Sleeves
Using 5½ mm. needles, cast on 33 (37,
41) sts. Work 7 rows in k. 1, p. 1 rib, inc.
3 sts. across last rib row – 36 (40, 44) sts.
Change to 6 mm. needles and cont. in
patt. as folls., at the same time inc. 1 st. at
each end of every foll. 4th row.

Rows 1 to 11: Work in st. st., beg. and ending with a k. row.
Rows 12 to 16: K.
These 16 rows form patt.
Cont. in patt., working incs. as before to 70 (74, 78) sts. When patt. has been completed four times, work 12 more rows st. st. Cast off loosely.

TO MAKE UP

Join left shoulder seam.

Neck Border

With right side facing and using 5½ mm. needles, pick up and k. 14 sts. along front left neck edge, k. across 18 sts. of front neck and pick up and k. 14 sts. along right front neck, 8 sts. along right back neck, k. across 26 sts. of back neck and pick up and k. 8 sts. along left back neck. Work in k. 1, p. 1 rib for 5 rows, then cast off ribwise. Join left shoulder seam and neck border. Sew in sleeves, matching centre of sleeve to shoulder line.
Join side and sleeve seams.

LONG VERSION

Back

Work as for Short version to **. Now cont. in patt. until work measures 51 (52, 52) cm. (20 (20½, 20¾) in.) ending with a wrong side row. Now complete as for Short version.

Front

Work as for Short version to **. Now cont. in patt. until work measures 47 (48, 50) cm. (18¾ (19, 19¾) in.) ending with a wrong side row. Now complete as for Short version.

Sleeves

Complete as for Short version.

TO MAKE UP

Complete as for Short version.

Navy Lark

MATERIALS

16 (17, 18) 50 g. balls Pingouin Coton Naturel 8 Fils; a pair each 3¼ mm. (no. 10) and 4 mm. (no. 8) knitting needles; a cable needle; 9 buttons.

TENSION

20 stitches and 26 rows to 10 cm. (4 in.) over stocking stitch using 4 mm. (no. 8) needles.

MEASUREMENTS

To fit bust 86 (91, 97) cm., 34 (36, 38) in.
Length from top of shoulder 79 (81, 83) cm., 31¼ (32, 32¾) in.
Sleeve seam (all sizes) 43 cm., 17 in.

ABBREVIATIONS

alt., alternate; beg., beginning; cont., continue; C10F, slip next 5 sts. on to a cable needle and hold at front of work, k. 5, then k. 5 from cable needle; dec., decrease; foll., following; inc., increase; k., knit; p., purl; patt., pattern; rem., remain(ing); rep., repeat; st(s)., stitch (es); st. st., stocking stitch; tog., together.

INSTRUCTIONS

Back

Using 3¼ mm. needles, cast on 102 (106, 110) sts. and work in k. 2, p. 2 rib as follows:
Row 1: K. 2 (p. 2, k. 2) to end.
Row 2: P. 2 (k. 2, p. 2) to end.
Rep. last 2 rows for 8 cm. (3 in.) ending with a 1st row.
Inc. Row: * Rib 5, inc. in next st., rep. from * to last 6 (10, 14) sts., rib 6 (10, 14) – 118 (122, 126) sts.
Change to 4 mm. needles and work in cable patt. as follows:
Row 1: K. 22 (24, 26), p. 4, k. 10, p. 4, k. 38, p. 4, k. 10, p. 4, k. 22 (24, 26).
Row 2: P. 22 (24, 26), k. 4, p. 10, k. 4, p.

Classic cotton cardigan in navy with cables is chic but casual and extremely versatile. You'd have to pay five times as much for it in a shop.
Easy.

38, k. 4, p. 10, k. 4, p. 22 (24, 26).
Rows 3 to 6: Rep. rows 1 and 2 twice.
Row 7: K. 22 (24, 26), p. 4, C10F, p. 4, k. 38, p. 4, C10K, p. 4, k. 22 (24, 26).
Row 8: As row 2.
Rows 9 to 14: Rep. rows 1 and 2 three times.
These 14 rows form the patt.
Work in patt. for 60 cm. (23½ in.) ending with a wrong side row.

To shape armholes Cast off 6 sts. at beg. of next 2 rows and 4 sts. at beg. of foll. 2 rows.
Dec. 1 st. at each end of the foll. 4 alt. rows – 90 (94, 98) sts.
Work straight until armhole measures 18 (19, 20) cm. (7(7½, 8) in.) ending with a wrong side row.

To shape neck Work 30 (32, 34) sts., cast off 30 sts., work to end. Working each side separately, dec. 1 st. at neck edge on every row until there are 26 sts. working 3 dec. over cable on last row – 23 sts. Cast off. Rejoin yarn and complete other side of neck to match.

Pocket lining (work 2)

Using 4 mm. needles, cast on 30 sts. and work in st. st. for 12 cm. (4¾ in.) ending with a p. row. Leave sts. on a spare needle.

Left front

Using 3¼ mm. needles, cast on 50 (50, 54) sts. and work in k. 2, p. 2 rib as given for back, ending with a 1st row and working 3 (5, 3) inc. evenly spaced – 53 (55, 57) sts.
Change to 4 mm. needles and work cable patt. as for back as follows:
Row 1: K. 22 (24, 26), p. 4, k. 10, p. 4, k. 13. This row sets the patt. Cont. in patt. until the 14th row of the 2nd patt. has been completed.

Work pocket opening as follows K. 10 (12, 14), slip the next 30 sts. on to a holder and in their place patt. across the 30 sts. of the pocket lining, k. to end.
Cont. in patt. until work measures 58 cm. (23 in.) from beg., ending with a right side row.
Dec. 1 st. at neck edge of next and every foll. 3rd row until work is same length as back to armhole, ending with a wrong side row.

To shape armhole Cont. to dec. at neck edge on every 3rd row as before, at the same time cast off 6 sts. at beg. of next row and 4 sts. at beg. of foll. alt. row, then dec. 1 st. at same edge on foll. 4 alt. rows. Now keep armhole edge straight, but cont. to dec. at neck edge as before until there are 26 sts. When armhole matches back to shoulder, work 3 dec. over cable on last wrong side row. Cast off.

Right front

Work as left front reversing all shapings and working 1st cable patt. row as follows: k. 13, p. 4, k. 10, p. 4, k. 22 (24, 26).
Work pocket opening row: K. 13, patt. over 30 sts. of pocket lining (slipping next 30 sts. of row on to a holder), k. to end.

Sleeves

Using 3¼ mm. needles, cast on 54 (58, 62) sts. and work in k. 2, p. 2 rib as given for back, but working last row as follows:
Inc. row: Rib 7 (9, 11), * inc. in next st., rib 2; rep. from * to last 5 (7, 9) sts., rib to end – 68 (72, 76) sts. Change to 4 mm. needles and work cable pattern as follows:
Row 1: K. 25 (27, 29), p. 4, k. 10, p. 4, k. 25 (27, 29).
Row 2: P. 25 (27, 29), k. 4, p. 10, k. 4, p. 25 (27, 29).
Rows 3 to 6: As rows 1 and 2 twice.
Row 7: K. 25 (27, 29), p. 4, C10F, p. 4, k. 25 (27, 29).
Row 8: As row 2.
Rows 9 to 14: As rows 1 and 2, three times.
These 14 rows form patt.
Cont. in patt. inc. 1 st. at each end of

every foll. 8th row until there are 84 (88, 92) sts. Cont. straight until work measures 43 cm. (17 in.) from beg., ending with a wrong side row.

To shape top Cast off 6 sts. at beg. of next 2 rows and 4 sts. at beg. of foll. 2 rows. Dec. 1 st. at each end of every alt. row until 32 sts. rem.
Cast off 6 sts. at beg. of next 2 rows.
Cast off rem. sts. working 4 dec. over cable.

Pocket edgings

Using 3¼ mm. needles, work over the 30 sts. of pocket opening in k. 2, p. 2 rib (beg. p. 2 on 1st and alt. rows) for 6 rows.
Cast off ribwise.

Front band

Using 3¼ mm. needles, cast on 12 sts. and work in k. 2, p. 2 rib for 8 rows.
** *Buttonhole row:* Rib 5, cast off 2, rib to end.
Next row: Rib 5, cast on 2, rib to end.
Work 16 more rows in rib. **
Rep. from ** to ** until 9 buttonholes have been worked. Now work in rib, omitting buttonholes, until band fits all round inner edge.
Cast off ribwise.

TO MAKE UP

Join shoulder seams. Set in sleeves. Join side and sleeve seams. Stitch down pocket linings and pocket tops. Sew on front band. Sew on buttons.

Peacock

Brilliant turquoise and huge cables translate into an evening look which would cost a fortune to buy.
Very easy.

MATERIALS

13 (14) 50 g. balls Pingouin Ruban; a pair each 7½ mm. (no. 1) and 6½ mm. (no. 3) needles; a cable needle.

Note Pingouin Ruban is available by mail order from Ries Wools, 243 High Holborn, London WC1V 7DZ.

Important: This yarn is circular knitted and pressed flat to give a smooth satin look. Because of the relatively heavy nature of this yarn, the garment will tend to drop in length when worn. For this reason it has additional width. Take all measurements with work hanging from needles. To prevent the yarn unravelling knot each cut end tightly. Fasten off all ends securely and don't sew seams too tightly.

TENSION

13 stitches and 17 rows to 10 cm. (4 in.) over stocking stitch using 7½ mm. (no. 1) needles.

MEASUREMENTS

To fit bust 86–91 (97–102) cm., 34–36 (38–40) in.
Approx. length when worn 63 cm., 25 in.

ABBREVIATIONS

alt., alternate; beg., beginning; C8, cable 8, slip next 4 sts. on to cable needle and hold at front, k. 4 then k. 4 from cable needle; cont., continue; dec., decrease; foll., following; inc., increase; k., knit; p., purl; patt., pattern; rem., remaining; rep., repeat; RS, right side; sl., slip; st(s)., stitch(es); st. st., stocking stitch; tog., together; WS, wrong side.

INSTRUCTIONS

Back (work side to side)
Beg. at right side seam, with 7½ mm. needles, cast on 82 sts. Work in patt.
Row 1 (RS): P. 10, * k. 8, p. 10, rep. from * to end.
Row 2: K. 10, * p. 8, k. 10, rep. from * to end.
Rows 3 to 8: Rep. rows 1 and 2 3 times.
Row 9: P. 10, * C8, p. 10, rep. from * to end.
Row 10: As row 2.
Rows 11 to 14: Rep. rows 1 and 2 twice.
These form patt.
Rep. 14 patt. rows once **.

To shape neck Keeping patt. correct, dec. 1 st. at beg. of next row and at the same edge on the foll. 3 rows – 78 sts.
Cont. in patt. until a total of 5 (6) patts. have been worked from beg., then rep. rows 1 to 10 once more. Inc. 1 st. at neck edge on next 4 rows – 82 sts. Rep. 14 patt. rows twice. Cast off loosely.

Front
Work as back to **.

To shape neck Dec. 1 st. at end of next row and at the same edge on the foll. 6 rows – 75 sts. Cont. in patt. until a total of 5 (6) patts. have been worked from beg. then rep. rows 1 to 7 once more. Inc. 1 st. at neck edge on next 7 rows – 82 sts. Rep. 14 patt. rows twice. Cast off loosely.

Neckband
Join right shoulder seam. With RS facing and using 6½ mm. needles, pick up and k. 48 (60) sts. evenly around front neck and 38 (50) sts. around back neck – 86 (110) sts. Work 5 rows in k. 1, p. 1 rib. Cast off in rib.

Armbands
Join left shoulder and neckband seam. Place markers on side edges of back and front 28 sts. from shoulder seams. With RS facing and using 6½ mm. needles, pick up and k. 56 sts. evenly between markers. Work 5 rows in k. 1, p. 1 rib. Cast off in rib.

TO MAKE UP

Do not press. Join side and armband seams.

Clashing Cables

MATERIALS

9 (10) 100 g. balls Hayfield Lugano Plain Mohair in shade chamonix; 6 (7) 50 g. balls Hayfield Grampian D.K. in black; 11 (12) 50 g. balls Hayfield Grampian Chunky in scarlet; a pair each 10 mm. (no. 000) and 12 mm. knitting needles; a cable needle.

TENSION

8 stitches and 11 rows to 10 cm. (4 in.) over stocking stitch using 12 mm. needles and 3 strands of yarn (see Note below).

MEASUREMENTS

To fit bust 81–86 (91–97) cm., 32–34 (36–38) in.
Length 87 (89) cm., 34¼ (35) in.
Sleeve seam (all sizes) 44 cm., 17¼ in.

ABBREVIATIONS

A., Grampian; B., Chunky; C8B, slip next 4 stitches on to cable needle to back of work, k. 4, then k. 4 from cable needle; C8F, slip next 4 stitches on to cable needle to front of work, k. 4, then k. 4 from cable needle; M., Lugano; dec., decrease; inc. increase; k., knit; p., purl; sl., slip; st(s)., stitch(es); tbl., through back of loop; tog., together.

Note Three strands of yarn are used together throughout – for main part use 1 strand of each yarn, called MAB; for cables only use 2 strands of M and one of A, called MMA; for collar only use 2 strands of B and 1 strand of A, called BBA. When working cables, use a separate second ball of M for each cable and strand the B loosely behind the cables.

INSTRUCTIONS

Back
Using 10 mm. needles and MAB cast on 53 (57) sts.
Row 1: K. 1, * p. 1, k. 1, repeat from * to end.
Row 2: P. 1, * k. 1, p. 1, repeat from * to end.
Repeat these 2 rows for 10 cm., ending with a 2nd row and inc. 1 st. at end of last row – 54 (58) sts. Change to 12 mm. needles and continue as follows:
Row 1: P. 13 (15) MAB, k. 8 MMA, p. 12 MAB, k. 8 MMA, p. 13 (15) MAB.
Row 2: K. 13 (15) MAB, p. 8 MMA, k. 12 MAB, p. 8 MMA, k. 13 (15) MAB. Repeat rows 1 and 2 twice more.
Row 7: P. 13 (15) MAB, with MMA C8F, p. 12 MAB, with MMA C8B, p. 13 (15) MAB.
Row 8: as row 2. Repeat rows 1 and 2 twice more. These 12 rows form the pattern; repeat them 4 times more.

To shape armholes Keeping pattern correct, cast off 5 sts. at beginning of next 2 rows – 44 (48) sts. Continue without shaping until armholes measure 23 (25) cm. (9 (10) in.), ending with a wrong side row.

To shape shoulders Cast off 12 sts. at beginning of next 2 rows. Leave remaining 20 (24) sts. on a spare needle.

Front
Work as given for back until 4 (6) rows less than back to shoulders.

To shape neck Next row: working in colours as set, p. 8 (10), k. 6, k. 2 tog., turn and leave remaining sts. on a spare needle. Continue on these sts., dec. one st. at neck edge on next 3 (5) rows. Cast off remaining 12 sts. Return to the sts. on spare needle; with right side facing sl. first 12 sts. on to a holder, rejoin yarns, k. 2 tog. tbl., k. 6, p. to end. Complete to match first side.

Sleeves
Using 10 mm. needles and MAB, cast on 23 (27) sts. and work in rib as on back for 7 cm. (2¾ in.), ending with a 2nd row and inc. 5 sts. evenly across last row – 28 (32) sts. Change to 12 mm. needles and beginning with a p. row continue in reverse st. st., inc. one st. at each end of 7th and every following 6th row until there are 38 (42) sts., then continue without shaping until sleeve measures 50 cm. (19½ in.) from beginning, ending with a k. row. Cast off loosely.

Collar
Join right shoulder seam. Using 10 mm. needles and BBA and with right side facing pick up and k. 6 (7) sts. down left front neck, k. front neck sts., pick up and k. 6 (7) sts. up right front neck, then k. back neck sts. Beginning with a p. row, continue in st. st. for 24 cm. (9½ in.). Cast off loosely.

TO MAKE UP

Do not press. Join left shoulder seam and collar, reversing seam on last 18 cm. (7 in.) of collar to turn over to right side. Sew in sleeves, sewing the last 6 cm. (2½ in.) of sleeve seams to the cast off sts. at armholes. Join side and sleeve seams.

Gingersnap

MATERIALS

11 (12) 50 g. balls Pingouin Typhon in main shade (M) Ecru (no. 05), 3 (3) 50 g. balls Pingouin Typhon contrast colour A (Noisetier, no. 53), 3 (3) 50 g. balls contrast colour B (Hanoi, no. 50), 1 (1) 50 g. ball contrast colour C (Banquise, no. 58), 1 (1) 50 g. ball contrast colour D (Bonbon, no. 02); a pair each of 5 mm. (no. 6) and 6 mm. (no. 4) knitting needles; 3 buttons.

Photograph shows sweater knitted in a different wool which has now been discontinued. Pingouin Typhon will knit up very slightly more bulky but will look even better. As an alternative wool, use Pingouin Orage: 7 (8) 50 g. balls in shade 152, 2 (2) 50 g. balls in shade 149 for contrast colour A, 2 (2) 50 g. balls in shade 150 for contrast colour B, 1 (1) 50 g. ball in shade 113 for contrast colour C, 1 (1) 50 g. ball in shade 137 for contrast colour D.

TENSION

16 stitches and 17 rows to 10 cm. (4 in.) over fair isle pattern using 6 mm. (no. 4) needles.

MEASUREMENTS

To fit bust 81–86 (91–97) cm., 32–34 (36–38) in., fitting loosely.
Back length 64 (65) cm., 25 (26) in.
Sleeve seam (both sizes) 42 cm., 16 in.

ABBREVIATIONS

alt., alternate; beg., beginning; cont., continue; dec., decrease; foll., following; inc., increase; k., knit; patt., pattern; p., purl; rem., remain(ing); rep., repeat; RS, right side; st(s)., stitch(es); st. st., stocking stitch; WS, wrong side.

INSTRUCTIONS

Back

With 5 mm. needles and M, cast on 95 (103) sts.
Work 12 rows: in k. 1, p. 1 rib beg. alt. rows p. 1 and inc. 3 sts. evenly across last row – 98 (106) sts. Change to 6 mm. needles. Cont. in st. st. in patt. from chart, twisting yarns together on WS when changing colour to prevent holes.
Row 1: reading 1st row of chart from right to left, k. first st., rep. 8 patt. sts. to last st., k. last st.
Row 2: reading 2nd row of chart from left to right, p. first st., rep. 8 patt. sts. to last st., p. last st.
Cont. in this way until back measures 40 cm. (15¾ in.) from cast-on edge, ending with a p. row.

To shape armholes Cast off 16 sts. at beg. of next 2 rows – 66 (74) sts. Patt. straight until work measures 64 (65) cm. (25 (25½) in.) from cast-on edge.

To shape shoulders Cast off 17 (18) sts. at beg. of next 2 rows. Cast off rem. 32 (38) sts.

Left front

With 5 mm. needles and M, cast on 58 (66) sts.
Work 12 rows in k. 1, p. 1 rib. Change to 6 mm. needles.
Next row: K. 50 (58) sts. as 1st row of chart, turn and leave rem. 8 sts. on a safety pin for button band. Cont in patt. from chart until work measures 23 cm. (9¼ in.) from cast-on edge, ending with p. row.

To shape front Keeping patt. correct, dec. 1 st. at end of next row and every foll. 4th (3rd) row until the same number of rows have been worked as on back to armholes, ending with a p. row.

To shape armholes Cont. to dec. at front edge as before and at the same time cast off 16 sts. at beg. of next row. Cont. with front decs. until 17 (18) sts. rem. Patt. straight until front matches back to shoulder. Cast off.

Right front

With 5 mm. needles and M, cast on 58 (66) sts.
Work 6 rows in k. 1, p. 1 rib.
1st buttonhole row: Rib 3, cast off 2 sts., rib to end.
2nd buttonhole row: Rib to last 3 sts., cast on 2 sts., rib 3. Rib 4 rows.
Next row: Rib 8 then slip these 8 sts. on to a safety pin for buttonhole band, change to 6 mm. needles and k. to end as 1st row of chart. Complete to match left front reversing shapings.

Sleeves

With 5 mm. needles and M, cast on 35 (41) sts.
Work 11 rows in k. 1, p. 1 rib beg. alt. rows p. 1.
Inc. row: Rib 2 (0), * inc. in next st., rib 4, rep. from * 5 (7) times, inc. in next st., rib 2 (0) – 42 (50) sts.
Change to 6 mm. needles. Cont. in patt. from chart inc. 1 st. at each end of every 3rd (4th) row until there are 78 (80) sts., working extra sts. into patt. Patt. straight until sleeve measures 52 cm. (20½ in.) from beg. Cast off.

Buttonhole band

With WS facing and using 5 mm. needles, rejoin M to sts. on safety pin. Cont. in rib working 2 more buttonholes as before, spaced 8.5 cm. (3¼ in.) apart, cont. in rib until band, when slightly stretched, will fit up right front and to centre back neck. Cast off.

Button band

With RS facing, work as for buttonhole band omitting buttonholes.

TO MAKE UP

Omitting ribbing, press pieces on WS using a warm iron and a dry cloth. Join shoulder seams. Join cast-off edges of sleeves to straight edges of armholes then join cast-off groups of 16 sts. to last 10 cm. (4 in.) of sides of sleeves. Join side and sleeve seams. Sew on front bands joining cast-off edges at centre back neck. Sew on buttons.

Florentine

MATERIALS

14 (15) 50 g. balls Patons Beehive Shetland Chunky in shade parma or 20 (21) 50 g. balls W. H. Smith Pure Wool Chunky; a pair each 5 mm. (no. 6) and 6 mm. (no. 4) knitting needles; 3 buttons.

TENSION

16 stitches and 20 rows to 10 cm. (4 in.) over stocking stitch using 6 mm. (no. 4) needles.

MEASUREMENTS

To fit bust 81–86 (91–97) cm., 32–34 (36–38) in.
Back length 64 (65) cm., 25 (26) in.
Sleeve seam (both sizes), 42 cm., 16 in.

ABBREVIATIONS

alt., alternate; beg., beginning; cont., continue; dec., decrease; foll., following; inc., increase; k., knit; patt., pattern; p., purl; rem., remain(ing); rep., repeat; RS, right side; st(s)., stitch(es); st. st., stocking stitch; WS, wrong side.

INSTRUCTIONS

Work in one colour only, as for Gingersnap, but when working sleeve shaping inc. on every 4th (4th) row instead of every 3rd (4th) row.

Maya

MATERIALS

10 50 g. balls Rowan Designer DK Cotton in main shade (254 orange), 8 50 g. balls contrast shade (251 ecru), 7 50 g. balls Rowan Designer DK Wool contrast shade (62 black); a pair each 6 mm. (no. 4) and 6½ mm. (no. 3) and 7 mm. (no. 2) knitting needles; a 6½ mm. (no. 3) circular knitting pin 40 cm. (16 in.) long.

TENSION

15 stitches and 22 rows to 10 cm. (4 in.) measured over garter stitch using 6½ mm. (no. 3) needles.

MEASUREMENTS

To fit bust 87–97 cm., 34–38 in.
Back length approx. 70 cm., 27½ in.
Sleeve seam approx. 45 cm., 18 in.

ABBREVIATIONS

alt., alternate; beg., beginning; cont., continue; dec., decrease; foll., following; g. st., garter stitch; inc., increase; k., knit; p., purl; patt., pattern; rem., remaining; rep., repeat; RS, right side; sl., slip; st(s)., stitch(es); st. st., stocking stitch; T2L, taking needle behind 1st st. k. into back of 2nd st. on left needle then k. into front of 1st st. and sl. both sts. off left needle tog.; T2R, k. into front of 2nd st. on left needle then k. into front of 1st st. and sl. both sts. off left needle tog.; tog., together; WS, wrong side.

Note Use yarn double throughout. M = 1 strand of orange and 1 strand of black tog. C = 2 strands of ecru tog. When working zigzag patt. and fair isle always twist yarns tog. on WS to prevent holes.

INSTRUCTIONS

Back

With 6 mm. needles and M, cast on 75 sts. Work 8 cm. (3 in.) in k. 1, p. 1 rib,

beg. alt. rows p. 1.
Inc. row: Rib 9, * inc. in next st., rib 18, rep. from * twice, inc. in next st., rib 8 – 79 sts. Change to 6½ mm. needles. Work 80 rows in g. st.
Inc. row: K. 13, * inc. in next st., k. 25; rep. from * once, inc. in next st., k. 13 – 82 sts. Change to 7 mm. needless. Cont. in zigzag patt. fastening off C at end of every RS row and rejoining it at beg. of foll. RS row.
Row 1 (WS): P 2 C, * 6 M, 2 C; rep. from * to end.

Row 2: With CT2R, * k 6 M, with C T2R; rep. from * to end.
Rows 3, 5 and 7: Sl. all C sts. purlwise with yarn at front and p. all M sts. with M. On rows 4, 6 and 8 when working T2L and T2R use colours of previous row.
Row 4: K. 1 M, * T2L, k. 4 M, T2R; rep. from * to last st., k. 1 M.
Row 6: K. 2 M, * T2L, k. 2 M, T2R, k. 2 M; rep. from * to end.
Row 8: K. 3 M, * T2L, T2R, k. 4 M; rep. from * to end, ending last rep. k. 3 M not k. 4 M.
Row 9: P. with M, inc. 1 st. at end – 83 sts. Cont. in st. st. in fair isle from chart.
Row 1 (RS): Reading row 1 of chart from right to left, k. all 42 sts. of chart, then reading row 1 from left to right miss st. before dotted line and k. rem. 41 sts.
Row 2: Reading row 2 of chart from right to left, p. all 42 sts. of chart, then reading row 2 from left to right miss st. before dotted line and p. rem. 41 sts. Cont. in this way until all 17 rows have been worked, p. 1 row M.
Next row: With M, k. to last 2 sts., k. 2 tog. – 82 sts. Work rows 1 to 8 of Zigzag patt. Cont. in M only **. Beg. p., st. st. 5 rows.

To shape shoulders Cast off 26 sts. at beg. of next 2 rows. Leave rem. 30 sts. on a spare needle.

Front

Work as back to **.

To shape neck 1st row (WS): P. 28, p. 2 tog., turn. Cont. on these 29 sts. only for 1st side. Beg. k. cont. in st. st. dec. 1 st. at neck edge on the next 3 rows. P. 1 row. Cast off rem. 26 sts.
Next row: With WS facing sl. centre 22 sts. on to a stitch holder, rejoin yarn to neck edge of rem. 30 sts., p. 2 tog., p. 28. Complete to match first side.

Sleeves

With 6 mm. needles and M, cast on 42 sts. Work 7 cm. (28 in.) in k. 1, p. 1 rib. Change to 6½ mm. needles. Cont. in g. st. inc. 1 st. at each end of 2nd row and every foll. 7th row until there are 54 sts. Work 2 rows straight.
Inc. row: K. 7, * inc. in next st., k. 12, rep.

Maya

from * twice, inc. in next st., k. 7 – 58 sts. Change to 7 mm. needles. Work rows 1 to 9 of Zigzag patt. 59 sts. Cont. in st. st. in fair isle from chart.

Row 1 (RS): Reading row 1 of chart from right to left and beg, at st. indicated, k. 30 sts., then reading row 1 from left to right miss st. before dotted line and k. 29 sts., ending at st. indicated. Work rows 2 to 17 of chart in this way inc. 1 st. at each end of every 4th row – 67 sts. P. 1 row M. Cast off loosely.

Collar

Join shoulder seams. With RS facing, using circular knitting pin and M, pick up and k. 4 sts. down left front neck, k. across 22 sts. at centre, pick up and k. 4 sts. up right front neck then k. across 30 sts. of back neck – 60 sts. Work 6 cm. (23½ in.) in rounds of k. 1, p. 1 rib. Cast off loosely in rib.

TO MAKE UP

With centre of cast-off edge of sleeves to shoulder seams, sew on sleeves. Join side and sleeve seams.

HIP BAND

MATERIALS

2 50 g. balls Rowan Designer DK cotton.

TENSION

As for sweater.

MEASUREMENTS

Width 14 cm., 55 in.

ABBREVIATIONS

As for sweater.

INSTRUCTIONS

With 4 mm. (no. 8) needles, cast on 180 sts. Work in k. 1, p. 1 rib for 14 cm. (55 in.). Cast off in rib.

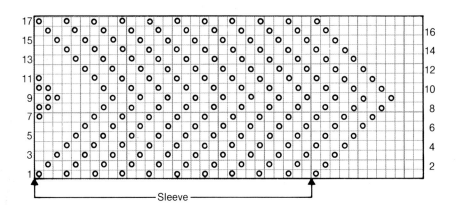

Sleeve

KEY □ main shade o contrast

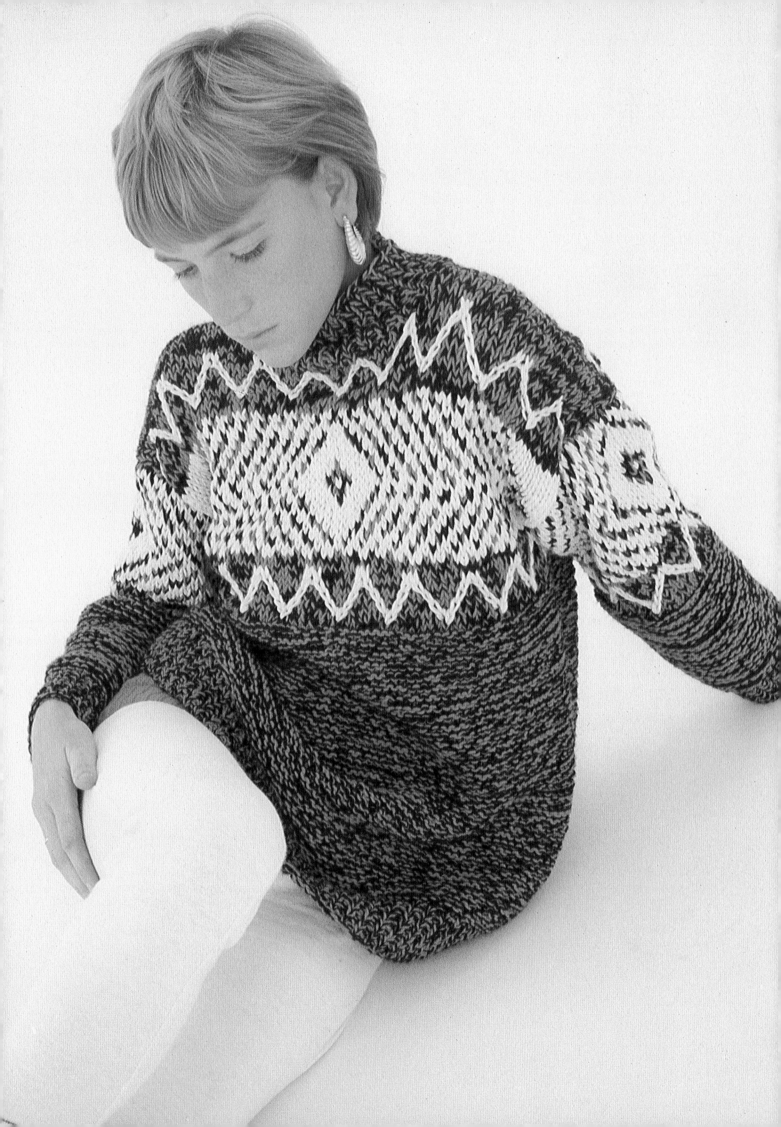

Oyster

MATERIALS

8 (8, 9) 50 g. balls Patons Cotton Perle; a pair each 3¾ mm. (no. 9) and 4 mm. (no. 8) knitting needles; a cable needle; 3 small buttons.

TENSION

24 sts. and 28 rows to 10 cm. (4 in.) over stocking stitch using 4 mm. (no. 8) needles.

MEASUREMENTS

To fit bust 86 (91, 97) cm., 34 (36, 38) in. Back length 52 (53, 54) cm., 20½ (21, 21¼) in.

ABBREVIATIONS

alt., alternate; beg., beginning; cont., continue; dec., decrease; foll., following; inc., increase; k., knit; p., purl; patt., pattern; rem., remaining; rep., repeat; RS, right side; sl., slip; st(s)., stitch(es); st. st., stocking stitch; tog., together; WS, wrong side.

INSTRUCTIONS

Back

With 3¾ mm. needles, cast on 129 (135, 141) sts. Work 7 cm. (2¾ in.) in k. 1, p. 1 rib, beg. WS rows p. 1 and ending with a RS row.
Inc. row: Rib 4 (2, 5), * inc. in next st., rib 5 (5, 4), inc. in next st., rib 5 (4, 4), rep. from * 9 (11, 12) times, inc. in next 1 (0, 1) st., rib 4 (1, 5) – 150 (159, 168) sts. Change to 4 mm. needles. Cont. in patt.
Row 1 (RS): K. 6 (7, 8), * p. 2, k. 8, p. 2, k. 6 (7, 8), rep. from * to end.
Row 2 and every foll. alt. row: P. 6 (7, 8), * k. 2, p. 8, k. 2, p. 6 (7, 8), rep. from * to end.
Row 3: As Row 1.
Row 5: As Row 1.
Row 7: K. 6 (7, 8), * p. 2, sl. next 4 sts. on to cable needle and hold at front, k. 4 then k. 4 from cable needle, p. 2, k. 6 (7, 8); rep. from * to end.
Row 9: As Row 1.
Row 10: As Row 2.
These 10 rows form patt. Cont. in patt. until work measures 32 cm. (12½ in.) from cast-on edge, ending with a WS row.

To shape armhole Row 1: Cast off 7 (8, 9) sts., [k. 2 tog., cast off 1 st.] 4 times, patt. to end.
Row 2: Cast off 7 (8, 9) sts., [p. 2 tog., cast off 1 st.] 4 times, patt. to end – 120 (127, 134) sts. Cast off 8 sts. at beg. of next 2 rows. Dec. 1 st. at each end of every row until 82 (87, 92) sts. rem. Patt. straight until back measures 18 (19, 20) cm. (7 (7½, 8) in.) from beg. of armhole shaping, ending with a WS row.

To shape neck Row 1: Patt. 22 (24, 26) sts., cast off next 38 (39, 40) sts., patt. to end. Cont. on last set of 22 (24, 26) sts. only and leave rem. sts. on a spare needle. Dec. 1 st. at neck edge on the next 3 rows. Cast off rem. 19 (21, 23) sts. loosely. With WS facing, rejoin yarn to neck edge of sts. on spare needle. Complete to match 1st side.

Front

Work as back until 1 less row has been worked than on back to armholes.
Dividing row (WS): Patt. 75 (80, 84) sts. and sl. these sts. on to a spare needle, patt. to end. Cont. on last set of 75 (79, 84) sts. only.

To shape armholes Row 1: As Row 1 of back armhole shaping – 60 (63, 67) sts. Patt. 1 row. Cast off 8 sts. at beg. of next row. Dec. 1 st. at armhole edge on the next 11 (12, 13) rows – 41 (43, 46) sts. Patt. straight until front measures 5 cm. (2 in.) less than back to shoulder, ending at centre front edge.

To shape neck Cast off 4 (4, 5) sts., [p. 2 tog., cast off 1 st.] 4 times, cast off next 6 sts., patt. to end. Dec. 1 st. at neck edge on the next 4 rows – 19 (21, 23) sts. Patt. straight until front matches back to shoulder. Cast off loosely. With RS facing, rejoin yarn to inner end of sts. on spare needle, cast off 0 (1, 0) st., patt. to end – 75 (79, 84) sts. Complete to match 1st side, reversing shapings.

Collar

With 3¾ mm. needles, cast on 129 sts. Work 30 rows in k. 1, p. 1 rib, beg. WS rows p. 1. Cast off loosely in rib.

Armbands

Join shoulder seams. With RS facing and using 3¾ mm. needles, pick up and k. 103 (109, 115) sts. evenly around armhole. Rib 7 rows. Cast off in rib.

Buttonhole band

With RS facing and using 3¾ mm. needles, pick up and k. 28 (30, 32) sts. evenly up right side of front opening. K. 1 row.
Buttonhole row: K. 6, * cast off 1 st., k. 8 (9, 10) *, rep. from * to * once, cast off 1 st., k. 3.
Next row: K. to end casting on 1 st. over each cast-off st. of last row. Cast off. Work button band to match, omitting buttonholes.

TO MAKE UP

Do not press. Join side and armband seams. With RS of collar to WS of sweater, and beg. and end at pick up row of front bands, sew cast-on edge of collar to neck edge. Overlap buttonhole band over button band and neaten lower edges. Sew on buttons.

Voile

MATERIALS

1 50 g. ball Pingouin Voile; a pair each 20 mm. and 9 mm. (no. 00) knitting needles; 2 press studs.

MEASUREMENTS

Length of bow before folding 52 cm., 20½ in.

TENSION

6 stitches and 12 rows to 10 cm. (4 in.) approx. using 20 mm. needles.

ABBREVIATIONS

k., knit; p., purl; RS, right side; sl., slip; st(s)., stitch(es); st. st., stocking stitch; tog., together.

INSTRUCTIONS

With 20 mm. needles cast on 14 sts. Work 42 rows in reverse st. st. (p. side is RS) and cast off.
With 9 mm. needles, cast on 6 sts. for centre band. Work 16 rows in st. st. Cast off. With 9 mm. needles, cast on 5 sts. for neckband. Work in st. st. until length will fit around neck. Cast off.

TO MAKE UP

Sew cast-on and cast-off edges of long strip tog. then wrap centre band around middle and sew in place. Sl. neckband through centre band. Sew on press studs to fasten at back of neck.

Aztec

MATERIALS

100 g. balls Alafoss Lopi Wool – 2 red (shade no. 78), 2 orange (shade no. 71), 2 navy (shade no. 118), 2 purple (shade no. 163), 2 khaki (shade no. 65), 1 wine red (shade no. 160), 1 cream (shade no. 51); a pair 6 mm. (no. 4) and a pair 6½ mm. (no. 3) knitting needles; a 6 mm. circular needle for collar.

Note Shade no. 189 can replace no. 71; shade no. 155 can replace no. 65.

These yarns are available by post from The Yarn Store, 8 Ganton Street (off Regent Street), London W1, tel. 01-734 4532, and from Colourspun, 18a Camden Road, Camden Town, London NW1 9HA, tel. 01-267 6317.

TENSION

14 stitches and 18 rows to 10 cm. (4 in.) over fair isle pattern using 6½ mm. (no. 3) needles.

MEASUREMENTS

One size only – to fit bust 87–97 cm., 34–38 in.
Length 71 cm., 28 in.
Sleeve seam 52 cm., 20½ in.

ABBREVIATIONS

cont., continue; dec., decrease; foll., following; inc., increase; k., knit; p., purl; RS, right side; st(s)., stitch(es); st. st., stocking stitch; tog., together; WS., wrong side.

INSTRUCTIONS

Back

With 6 mm. needles and khaki yarn, cast on 69 sts. Work in k. 1, p. 1 rib for 7 cm. (2¾ in.), working 5 incs. evenly along last rib row – 74 sts. Change to 6½ mm. needles. ** Now work fair isle from chart, working rows 1 to 78 once, then working rows 11 to 24 again, using khaki instead of orange. Now work rows

Richness of colour and pattern form primitive prints. The mood is tribal with clashing colour combinations.

39 to 44 again, using red instead of khaki and purple instead of orange. Now work rows 45 and 46, but at the same time shape back neck.

To shape back neck K. 23, k. 2 tog., turn; work on these sts. only.
Next row: P. 2 tog., p. to end. Cast off.

Slip the middle 24 sts. on to a spare needle. Rejoin yarn and complete other side of neck to match.

Front

Exactly as back to **.
Now work fair isle from chart, working rows 1 to 78 once, then working rows 11 to 20 again, using khaki instead of orange.
Cont. to work fair isle as for back, but shape front neck.

To shape front neck K. 27, k. 2 tog., turn; work on these sts. only. Dec. 1 st. at neck edge on every row to 23 sts. When fair isle matches back, cast off. Slip the centre 16 sts. on to a spare needle. Rejoin yarn and complete other side of neck to match.

Sleeves

With 6 mm. needles and khaki, cast on 31 sts. Work in k. 1, p. 1 rib for 7 cm. (2¾ in.), working 7 incs. evenly along last rib row – 38 sts. Change to 6½ mm. needles and navy. Work 2 rows in st. st. then work fair isle as below, but inc. 1 st. at each end of every foll. 4th row to 68 sts. Now work fair isle from chart, working rows 39 to 50 once: use red instead of khaki and purple instead of orange. Now work rows 1 to 38. Finally, work rows 11 to 24 again, using khaki instead of orange. Cast off. Join shoulder seams.

Collar

Using a 6 mm. circular needle and orange yarn, pick up and k. 12 sts. along left front neck, k. across the 16 sts. of front neck, pick up and k. 12 sts. along right front neck, then k. across the 24 sts. of back neck. Work in rounds of k. 1 p. 1 rib until the 16th round has been completed, then cast off ribwise.

TO MAKE UP

Press according to instructions on ball band. Sew on sleeves, allowing for an armhole of 24 cm. (9¼ in.). Join side seams and sleeve seams. Press all seams.

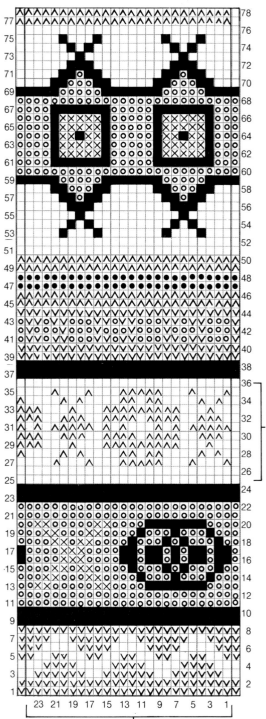

For rows 25–36, repeat the first 16 sts. only

Pattern repeat of 24 stitches, with one selvedge stitch at each end of every row

KEY □ red V khaki ■ navy o orange
X cream ∧ purple ● wine red

Double Cream

MATERIALS

10 (11) 50 g. balls Pingouin Boule de Coton or 8 (9) 50 g. balls Pingouin Coton Mousse; 10 (11) 50 g. balls Pingouin Tricotine; a pair of 7 mm. (no. 2) knitting needles.

TENSION

12 stitches and 19 rows to 10 cm. (4 in.) over pattern.

MEASUREMENTS

To fit bust 81–86 (91–97) cm., 32–34 (36–38) in., fitting very loosely. Actual garment measurement 100 (110) cm., 39 (43) in.
Length (all sizes) 58 cm., 22¾ in.
Sleeve seam (all sizes) 29 cm., 11 in.

ABBREVIATIONS

beg., beginning; inc., increasing; k., knit; p., purl; patt., pattern; rep., repeat; rev. st. st., reverse stocking stitch; st(s)., stitch(es); st. st., stocking stitch.

INSTRUCTIONS

Note Use 1 strand of Boule de Coton or Coton Mousse and 1 strand of Tricotine together throughout the sweater.

Back and front alike
Cast on 60 (66) sts. Work in patt. thus:
Rows 1 to 6: Beg. with a p. row, work 6 rows in rev. st. st.
Rows 7 to 10: Beg. with a k. row, work 4 rows in st. st. These 10 rows form patt. Rep. the 10 patt. rows 10 times more. Cast off loosely.

Sleeves
Cast on 48 (54) sts. Work in patt. as given for back, inc. 1 st. at each end of every 8th row until there are 58 (64) sts. Cont. in patt. until the 6th row of the 6th patt. has been worked. Cast off loosely.

TO MAKE UP

Join shoulder seams leaving centre 25 cm. (9¾ in.) open for neck. Join side seams leaving top 24 (27) cm. (9¼ (10½) in.) open for armholes. Join sleeve seams. Set in sleeves.

DOUBLE CREAM JUNIOR

MATERIALS

4 (5, 5, 6) 50 g. balls Pingouin Boule de Coton or 3 (4, 4, 5) balls of Pingouin Coton Mousse and 4 (5, 5, 6) 50 g. balls Pingouin Tricotine; a pair of 7 mm. (no. 2) knitting needles.

TENSION

12 stitches and 19 rows to 10 cm. (4 in.) over pattern.

MEASUREMENTS

To fit chest 56 (61, 66, 71) cm., 22 (24, 26, 28) in.
Length 32 (37, 42, 42) cm., 12½ (14½, 16½, 16½) in.
Sleeve length 19 (19, 24, 24) cm., 7½ (7½, 9½, 9½) in.

ABBREVIATIONS

beg., beginning; inc., increasing; k., knit; p., purl; patt., pattern; rep., repeat; rev. st. st., reverse stocking stitch; st(s)., stitch(es); st. st., stocking stitch.

INSTRUCTIONS

Note Use 1 strand of Boule de Coton or Coton Mousse and 1 strand of Tricotine together throughout the sweater.

Back and front alike
Cast on 35 (38, 41, 44) sts. Work in patt. as given for woman's sweater until the 10 patt. rows have been worked a total of 6 (7, 8, 8) times. Cast off loosely.

Sleeves
Cast on 20 (23, 26, 29) sts. Work in patt. inc. 1 st. at each end of every 6th row until there are 28 (31, 34, 37) sts. Cont. in patt. until the 6th row of the 4th (4th, 5th, 5th) patt. has been worked. Cast off loosely.

TO MAKE UP

Join shoulder seams leaving centre 18 (19, 20, 21) cm. (7 (7½, 8, 8½) in.) open for neck. Join side seams leaving top 12 (13, 14, 15.5) cm. (4¾ (5, 5½, 6) in.) open for armholes. Join sleeve seams. Set in sleeves.

Violet

MATERIALS

16 (17, 18) 50 g. balls Laines Anny Blatt, Look'Anny; a pair each 7 mm. (no. 2) and 6½ mm. (no. 3) knitting needles.

Note Look'Anny by Laines Anny Blatt is available by mail order from Ries Wools, 243 High Holborn, London WC1V 7DZ.
Important: This yarn is circular knitted and pressed flat to give a smooth satin look. Because of the relatively heavy nature of this yarn, the garment will tend to drop in length when worn. For this reason it has additional width. Take all measurements with work hanging from needles. To prevent the yarn unravelling knot each cut end tightly. Fasten off all ends securely and don't sew seams too tightly.

TENSION

10 stitches to 7 cm. (2¾ in.) and 9 rows to 5 cm. (2 in.) over pattern using 7 mm. (no. 2) needles.

MEASUREMENTS

To fit bust 86 (91, 97) cm., 34 (36, 38) in.
Length from shoulder 62 (63, 64) cm., 24 (24¾, 25) in.
Sleeve seam (all sizes) 34 cm., 13 in.

ABBREVIATIONS

cont., continue; dec., decrease; foll., following; in., inches; inc., increase; k.,

Parma violet makes a stunning choice for evening in this ribbon top which you can wear belted and bloused or seductively loose. Easy.

knit; K1B, insert point of right-hand needle through centre of stitch 1 row below next stitch on left-hand needle and k. it; p., purl; patt., pattern; rem., remaining; rep., repeat; RS, right side; sl., slip; st(s)., stitch(es); st. st., stocking stitch; tog., together; WS, wrong side.

INSTRUCTIONS

Back
With 7 mm. needles, cast on 84 (89, 94) sts. Work in patt.
Row 1: K.
Row 2 (RS): P. 4, * k.1B, p. 4, rep. from * to end.
These two rows form patt. **. Cont. until back measures 60 (61, 62) cm. (23½ (24, 24½) in.) ending with a WS row.

To shape neck *Row 1:* patt. 24 (26, 29) sts., k. 2 tog., turn. Cont. on these sts. only for first side and leave rem. sts. on a spare needle. Dec. 1 st. at neck edge on next 3 rows. Cast off rem. 22 (24, 27) sts. With RS facing, sl. centre 32 (33, 32) sts. on to a stitch holder, rejoin yarn to inner end of rem. sts., k. 2 tog., patt. to end. Complete to match first side.

Front
Work as back to **. Cont. in patt. until front measures 54 (55, 56) cm. (21¼ (21¾, 22¼) in.), ending with a WS row.

To shape neck *Row 1:* Patt. 30 (32, 35) sts., k. 2 tog., turn. Cont. on these sts. only for first side and leave rem. sts. on a spare needle. Dec. 1 st. at neck edge on next 9 rows. Patt. straight until front matches back to shoulder. Cast off. With RS facing, sl. centre 20 (21, 20) sts. on to a stitch holder, rejoin yarn to inner end of rem. sts., k. 2 tog., patt. to end. Complete to match first side.

Sleeves
With 7 mm. needles, cast on 39 (44, 49) sts. Work in patt. as given for back inc. 1 st. at each end of 3rd and every foll. 4th row until there are 69 (74, 79) sts., working inc. sts. into patt. Patt. 2 rows. Cast off loosely.

Neckband
Join right shoulder seam. With RS facing and using 6½ mm. needles, pick up and k. 16 sts. down left front neck, patt. across 20 (21, 20) sts. at centre front, pick up and k. 16 sts. up right front neck and 6 sts. down right back neck, patt. across 32 (33, 32) sts. at centre back neck then pick up and k. 6 sts. up left back neck – 96 (98, 96) sts. Work 5 rows in k. 1, p. 1 rib. Cast off in rib.

TO MAKE UP

Join left shoulder and neckband seam. With centre of cast-off edge of sleeves to shoulder seams and beg. and ending 24 (26, 28) cm. (9½ (10¼, 11) in.) from shoulder seams, sew on sleeves. Join side and sleeve seams.

Watercolour

Pure silk sweater in gentle glowing colours which has a subtle 'squares' theme and a square neckline. Although the silk is fine, the fair isle is simple but interesting to work.
Easy.

MATERIALS

4 (4) 50 g. balls Maxwell Cartlidge 100% pure silk in main shade – avocado (M), 1 (1) ball in contrast shade – ocean (A), 2 (3) balls ivory (B), 1 (2) balls rosedust (D), and 2 (2) hanks mink (C); a pair each 2¼ mm. (no. 13) and 3 mm. (no. 11) Aero knitting needles.

The yarn is available by mail order only; for price list send s.a.e. to Maxwell Cartlidge, PO Box 33, Colchester, Essex.

TENSION

32 stitches and 32 rows to 10 cm. (4 in.) square in pattern using 3 mm. (no. 11) needles.

MEASUREMENTS

To fit bust 81–86 (91–97) cm., 32–34 (36–38) in.; actual size 94 (107) cm., 37 (42) in.
Length (all sizes) 53 (55) cm., 21 (21½) in.
Sleeve seam (all sizes) approx. 41 cm., 16 in.

ABBREVIATIONS

alt., alternate; beg., beginning; cont., continue; dec., decreas(e)ing; foll., following; inc., increas(e)ing; k., knit; p., purl; patt., pattern; rem., remain(ing); rep., repeat; sl., slip; sts., stitches; t.b.l., through back loops; tog., together; 0, no stitches.

Note Figures in brackets refer to larger sizes; where only one figure is given, this refers to all sizes.

INSTRUCTIONS

Back

With 2¼ mm. needles and M, cast on 145 (165) sts. Work 6 cm. k. 1, p. 1 rib, beg. alt. rows p. 1.
Inc. row: Rib 17 (20), * inc. in next st., rib

15 (17); rep. from * to last 16 (19) sts., inc. in next st., rib to end. 153 (173) sts. Change to 3 mm. needles and cont. in patt. thus:
Row 1: With M, k.
Row 2: With M, p.
Rows 3 and 4: As rows 1 and 2.
Row 5: K. 3 M, (7 A, 3 M) to end.
Row 6: P. as row 5.
Rows 7 and 8: As rows 5 and 6.
Rows 9 and 10: As rows 1 and 2.
Rows 11 and 12: With B, as rows 1 and 2.
Rows 13 to 16: As rows 1 to 4.
Row 17: K. 3 (4) M, (3 B, 3 M) to last 0 (1) st., 0 (1) M.
Row 18: P. as row 17.
Rows 19 and 20: As rows 17 and 18.
Rows 21 to 24: As rows 1 to 4.
Rows 25 and 26: As rows 11 and 12.
Rows 27 and 28: With C, as rows 1 and 2.
Rows 29 and 30: As rows 11 and 12.
Row 31: K. 3 B, (7 D, 3 B) to end.
Row 32: P. as row 31.
Rows 33 and 34: As rows 31 and 32.
Row 35: K. 3 B, (2 D, 3 B) to end.
Row 36: P. as row 35.
Rows 37 to 40: As rows 31 to 34.
Rows 41 to 46: As rows 25 to 30.
Rows 47 and 48: As rows 1 and 2.
Row 49: K. 2 M, (1 A, 3 M) to last 3 sts., 1 A, 2 M.
Row 50: P. as row 49.
Rows 51 and 52: As rows 49 and 50.
Rows 53 to 56: As rows 9 to 12.
Row 57: K. 3 (4) D, (3 M, 3 D) to last 0 (1) st., 0 (1) D.
Row 58: P. as row 57.
Row 59: K. 3 (4) M, (3 D, 3 M) to last 0 (1) st., 0 (1) M.
Row 60: P. as row 59.
Rows 61 and 62: As rows 57 and 58.
Rows 63 and 64: As rows 11 and 12.
These 64 rows form the patt. Now work rows 1 to 28. Work should measure approx. 35 cm. (13¾ in.).

To shape armholes Keeping patt. correct, cast off 8 (9) sts. at beg. of next 2 rows. Dec. 1 st. at both ends of next row and foll. alt. rows to 113 (125) sts. ** Patt. 31 rows straight, thus ending after wrong-side row.

To shape neck and shoulders Next row: Patt. 38 (44), turn and leave rem. sts. on spare needle.
Next row: P. 2 tog., patt. to end. Cast off 11 (13) sts. at beg. of next row and foll. alt. row *at the same time* dec. 1 st. at neck edge on next 3 rows. Work 1 row. Cast off. With right side facing, sl. centre 37 sts. on to spare needle. Rejoin yarn to rem. sts. and work to match 1st side, reversing shapings.

Front

Work as back to **. Patt. 1 row, thus ending after wrong-side row.

To shape neck Next row: Patt. 34 (40), turn and leave rem. sts. on spare needle. Cont. in patt. until front matches back to shoulder, ending after wrong-side row.

To shape shoulder Cast off 11 (13) sts. at beg. of next row and foll. alt. row. Work 1 row. Cast off. with right side facing, sl. centre 45 sts. on to spare needle. Rejoin yarn to rem. sts. and

work to match 1st side, reversing shapings.

Sleeves

With 2¼ mm. needles and M, cast on 67 sts. and work 7 cm. k. 1, p. 1 rib, as back. *Inc. row:* Rib 8, (inc. in next st., rib 1) 25 times, inc. in next st., rib to end. 93 sts. Change to 3 mm. needles. Beg. with row 47, cont. in patt. as 1st size back, *at the same time* inc. 1 st. at both ends of 11th row and every foll. 14th (8th) row to 105 (115) sts., taking inc. sts. into patt. Cont. straight until work measures approx. 41 cm. (16¼ in.), ending after 28th patt. row.

To shape top Cast off 8 (9) sts. at beg. of next 2 rows. Dec. 1 st. at both ends of next row and foll. alt. rows to 65 (69) sts., then at both ends of foll. 3rd rows to 57 (59) sts. With M only, cont. dec. as before on foll. 3rd rows to 51 (55) sts.
Next row: K. 1, then k. 2 tog. to end. Cast off.

Neckband

Join right shoulder seam. With right side facing, using 2¼ mm. needles and M, pick up and k. 33 sts. down left front neck, 1 st. at left corner, k. across front sts., pick up and k. 1 st. at right corner, 33 sts. up right front neck, 6 sts. down right back neck, k. across back sts. dec. 1 st. at centre and pick up and k. 6 sts. up left back neck. 161 sts.
Next row: K. 1, (p. 1, k. 1) 39 times, p. 2 tog., p. 1, p. 2 tog., t.b.l., k. 1, (p. 1, k. 1) 20 times, p. 2 tog., p. 1, p. 2 tog. t.b.l., k. 1, (p. 1, k. 1) to end. Work 8 more rows rib, dec. 1 st. at each side of front corner sts. and keeping these corner sts. in st. st. Cast off in rib, dec. as before.

TO MAKE UP

Press pieces on wrong side with a warm iron and a damp cloth. Join left shoulder and neckband seam. Join side and sleeve seams. Sew in sleeves.

Telling Tails

MATERIALS

16 (17, 18) 50 g. balls Pingouin Iceberg for jacket; 8 (9) 50 g. balls Pingouin Iceberg for skirt; a pair 6 mm. (no. 4) knitting needles; 2 buttons; 2 safety pins for jacket; a pair 5½ mm. (no. 5) knitting needles; waist length of elastic for skirt.

TENSION

13 stitches and 19 rows to 10 cm. (4 in.) over stocking stitch using 6 mm. (no. 4) needles.
12 stitches and 16 rows to 10 cm. (4 in.) over stocking stitch using 5½ mm. (no. 5) needles.

MEASUREMENTS

To fit bust 86 (91, 97) cm., 34 (36, 38) in. (fitting loosely).
Length approx. 50 (52, 54) cm., 19½ (20½, 21¼) in. (not counting flap at back).
Sleeve seam (all sizes) 52 cm., 20½ in.
To fit hips 87–91 (91–97) cm., 34–36 (36–38) in.
Length 46 (48) cm., 18 (19) in.

ABBREVIATIONS

alt., alternate; beg., beginning; cont., continue; dec., decrease; foll., following; g. st., garter stitch; inc., increase; k., knit; p., purl; rep., repeat; RS, right side; st(s)., stitch(es); st. st., stocking stitch; tog., together; WS, wrong side.

INSTRUCTIONS

JACKET

Back
To shape back point Using 6 mm. needles cast on 1 st. K. inc. twice into st. (3 sts.).
Next row: K. 3.
Next row: Inc. into 1st st., k. 1, inc. into last st. (5 sts.).
Next row: K. 5.

Violet jacket with a 'tail' at the back has asymmetric front edges and a matching, easily made ribby skirt. The jacket is stocking stitch with garter stitch borders.
Easy.

Next row: Inc. into 1st st., k. 3, inc. into last st. (7 sts.).
Next row: K. 7. Cont. in this way to 11 sts.
Next row: K. 3, inc. into next st., k. to last 4 sts., inc. into next st., k. 3.
Next row: K. across all sts.

Rep. last 2 rows until 15 sts. are on the needle.
Next row: K. 15.
Next row: (RS facing) K. 3, inc. into next st., k. to last 4 sts., inc. into next st., k. 3.
Next row: K. 3, inc. into next st., p. to last 4 sts., inc. into next st., k. 3.
Rep. last 2 rows until 47 (51, 55) sts. are on the needle keeping the g. st. border correct and ending with a WS row. Cast on 9 sts. at beg. of next 2 rows – 65 (69, 73) sts. Working the 9 sts. at each end of row in g. st. and the rem. sts. in st. st. as set, work 6 more rows. Starting with a k. row, cont. across all row in st. st. for 86 (90, 94) rows.

To shape back neck *Next row:* (RS facing) K. 20 (22, 24) sts., cast off next 25 sts., k. to end, turn, and work on this last set of sts. only.
Next row: P. to last 2 sts., p. 2 tog. (neck edge) – 19 (21, 23) sts. Cast off.
With WS facing rejoin yarn to rem. sts., p. 2 tog., p. to end – 19 (21, 23) sts. Cast off.

Left front
Using 6 mm. needles cast on 32 (36, 40) sts. K. 4 rows.
Next row: K. to last 5 sts., inc. into next st., k. to end – 33 (37, 41) sts.
Next row: K.
Now work in st. st. with g. st. border at edge inside, but inc. at inside edge as follows:
Row 1: (RS facing) K. to last 5 sts., inc. into next st., k. to end.
Row 2: K. 4, p. to end.
Rep. these last 2 rows until 50 (54, 58) sts. are on the needle, ending with a WS row. **
Now work straight in st. st. for 4 more rows, still working the 4 sts. at inside edge in g. st.

To shape front neck Cont. to work the 4 sts. at inside edge on every row in g. st. and the rest of row in st. st. as set, *at the same time,* dec. 1 st. over the 2 sts. next to the 4 g. st. sts. on every alt. row until 25 (27, 29) sts. remain. Now dec. 1 st. over these 2 sts. on every row until 22 (24, 26) sts. remain. Cast off all sts. except for the 4 sts. in g. st. Leave these sts. on a safety pin.

Right front

Work as for left front, reversing shaping to **. Now work straight in st. st. for 4 more rows still working the 4 sts. at inside edge in g. st., *at the same time* work two buttonholes over the first two of these rows as follows:

Row 1: (RS facing) K. 4, cast off next 2 sts., k. 12, cast off next 2 sts., k. to end.
Row 2: P. to cast off sts., cast on 2 sts., p. 12, cast on 2 sts., k. 4.

Now complete to match left front reversing all shapings.

Sleeves (make 2)

Using 6 mm. needles cast on 36 (38, 40) sts. K. 6 rows. Starting with a k. row, work in st. st., but inc. 1 st. at each end of every foll. 5th row until there are 66 (68, 70) sts. on the needle. Work straight in st. st. until sleeve measures 52 cm. (20½ in.) from cast-on edge, ending with a WS row. Cast off loosely.

TO MAKE UP

Press all pieces except garter stitch with a warm iron and a damp cloth on the reverse side. Either join shoulder seams together or undo cast-off edges and graft each shoulder seam together (except for the 4 sts. in garter stitch on each side which form neckband).

Neckband

Slip the 4 sts. in garter stitch on right front on to a 6 mm. needle and work straight until strip fits to centre back neck. Rep. for left front. Graft the two sets of 4 sts. together or cast off and stitch in place.

To complete

With centre of cast-off edges of sleeves to shoulder seams, sew sleeves in position. Join side and sleeve seams. Sew on buttons to correspond with buttonholes. Press all seams.

SKIRT

Front and back (alike)

Using 5½ mm. needles cast on 72 (82) sts. and work in rib pattern as follows:
Row 1: (WS facing) K. 2, (p. 3, k. 2) to end.
Row 2: P. 2 (k. 3, p. 2) to end.

These two rows form the pattern and are repeated throughout. Cont. straight in patt. until skirt measures 46 (48) cm. (18 (19) in.) from cast-on edge (or skirt length required), ending with a WS row. Cast off in rib pattern.

TO MAKE UP

Join side seams. Press all seams. Herringbone stitch elastic to waist and adjust to fit.

Gold Strike

MATERIALS

21 (22, 23) 25 g. balls Twilleys Gold-fingering in gold WG2 (used double); a pair 5½ mm. (no. 5) and a pair 6½ mm. (no. 3) knitting needles; a cable needle.

TENSION

17 stitches and 24 rows to 10 cm. (4 in.) over st. st. on 6½ mm. (no. 3) needles with yarn used double.

MEASUREMENTS

To fit bust 87 (91, 97) cm., 34 (36, 38) in.
Length 54 (55, 56) cm., 21¼ (21½, 22) in.
Sleeve seam (all sizes) 48 cm., 19 in.

ABBREVIATIONS

alt., alternate; cont., continue; C4F, slip the next 4 sts. on to cable needle and hold at front of work, k. 4, then k. 4 from cable needle; dec., decrease; foll., following; inc., increase; k., knit; p., purl; patt., pattern; p.s.s.o., pass slip stitch over; rep., repeat; RS, right side; s.k.p.o., slip one, knit one, pass the slip stitch over; st(s)., stitch(es); tog., together.

INSTRUCTIONS

Back
With 5½ mm. needles, using yarn double, cast on 85 (91, 97) sts. Work in k. 1 p. 1 rib for 7 rows, working 7 incs. evenly along last rib row – 92 (98, 104) sts.
Change to 6½ mm. needles. With RS facing, work the foll. cable patt.:
Row 1: P. 6 (3, 6), * k. 8, p. 4, rep. from *, ending last rep. p. 6 (3, 6).
Row 2: K. the k. sts. and p. the p. sts. as they face you. Rep. these 2 rows twice more.
Row 7: P. 6 (3, 6), * C4F, p. 4, rep. from *, ending last rep. p. 6 (3, 6).
Row 8: As row 2.
These 8 rows form patt. Cont. to work

The beautiful gold yarn (knitted double) makes a stunning cabled classic for evening. You could try knitting it longer for a more sophisticated look, and using the head band as a hipline band, knotted at the side (cast on more stitches and knit it a bit wider).

patt., but inc. 1 st. at each end of every foll. 10th row to 100 (106, 112) sts. ** When patt. has been worked 12 times in all, work 2 (6, 10) more rows then shape neck.

To shape neck Patt. 32 (35, 38), k. 2 tog., turn. Work on these sts. only. Dec. 1 st. at neck edge on every row to 24

(27, 30) sts., then cast off, working 4 decs. over cable as you cast off – 20 (23, 26) sts. Slip the centre 32 sts. on to a spare needle, working 4 decs. over centre cable by working p.s.s.o. twice, then s.k.p.o. twice – 28 sts. Rejoin yarn and complete other side of neck to match.

Front

Exactly as back to **. When patt. has been worked 11 times in all, shape neck.

To shape neck Patt. 38 (41, 44), k. 2 tog., turn. Work on these sts. only. Dec. 1 st. at neck edge on every row to 24 (27, 30) sts., then cast off, working 4 decs. over cable as you cast off – 20 (23, 26) sts. Slip the centre 16 sts. on to a spare needle, working 4 decs. over centre cable by working p.s.s.o., twice, then s.k.p.o. twice. 12 sts. on spare needle. Rejoin yarn and complete other side of neck to match.

Sleeves

With 5½ mm. needles, using yarn double, cast on 37 (37, 43) sts. Work in k. 1 p. 1 rib for 7 cm. (2¾ in.), working 9 incs. evenly along last rib row – 46 (46,

52) sts. Change to 6½ mm. needles, and work the foll. patt:
Row 1: K. 3 (3, 6), * p. 4, k. 8, rep. from * to last 7 sts., p. 4, k. 3 (3, 6).
Cont. to work patt. as set for back, but inc. 1 st. at each end of 6th and every foll. 4th row to 80 (80, 86) sts., working extra sts. into cable patt.
When length measures 48 cm. (19 in.) from beg., cast off. Join left shoulder seam.

NECKBAND

With 5½ mm. needles, using yarn double, pick up and k. 18 sts. along left front neck, k. across the 12 sts. of front neck, then pick up and k. 18 sts. along right front neck; now pick up and k. 6 sts. along right back neck, k. across the 28 sts. of back neck, then pick up and k. 6 sts. along left back neck. Work in k. 1 p. 1 rib for 6 rows, then cast off ribwise.

TO MAKE UP

Join right shoulder seam and neckband. Sew on sleeves, allowing for an armhole of 19 (19, 20) cm. (7½ (7½, 8) in.). Join

side seams and sleeve seams. Do not press.

Headband

MATERIALS

2 25 g. balls Twilleys Goldfingering in gold WG2 (used double); a pair 5½ mm. (no. 5) knitting needles.

ABBREVIATIONS AND TENSION

As for sweater.

MEASUREMENTS

Length 58 cm., 23 in.
Width 8 cm., 3 in.

INSTRUCTIONS

With 5½ mm. needles and yarn used double, cast on 141 sts. Work in k. 1, p. 1 rib for 8 cm. (3 in.), then cast off in rib.

Cool Neutral

MATERIALS

8 (9, 9) 50 g. balls Pingouin Coton Naturel 8 Fils; a pair each 3¼ mm. (no. 10) and 3¾ mm. (no. 9) knitting needles; 6 buttons.

TENSION

22 stitches and 30 rows to 10 cm. (4 in.) over pattern using 3¾ mm. (no. 9) needles.

MEASUREMENTS

To fit bust 86 (91, 97) cm., 34 (36, 38) in. Length 59 (60, 61) cm., 23¼ (23½, 24) in.

ABBREVIATIONS

alt., alternate; beg., beginning; cont., continue; dec., decrease; foll., following; inc., increase; k., knit; p., purl; patt., pattern; rep., repeat; st(s)., stitch(es); tog., together.

INSTRUCTIONS

Back
With 3¼ mm. needles, cast on 98 (104, 110) sts. and work 18 rows k. 1, p. 1 rib, inc. 6 sts. evenly along last rib row – 104 (110, 116) sts. Change to 3¾ mm. needles and patt.
Row 1: K.
Row 2: P.
Row 3: K. 2, * p. 4, k. 2; rep. from * to end.
Row 4: P. 2, * k. 4, p. 2; rep. from * to end.
Rows 5 and 6: As rows 3 and 4.
Row 7: K.
Row 8: P.
Row 9: P. 3, * k. 2, p. 4; rep. from * to last 5 sts., k. 2, p. 3.
Row 10: K. 3, * p. 2, k. 4; rep. from * to last 5 sts., p. 2, k. 3.
Rows 11 and 12: As rows 9 and 10.
These 12 rows form patt. Cont. in patt. until work measures 38 cm. (15 in.) from beg., ending with a wrong side row.

To shape armholes Cast off 8 sts. at beg. of next 2 rows and 5 sts. at beg. of foll. 2 rows. Now dec. 1 st. at each end of foll. 5 alt. rows – 68 (74, 80) sts. Cont. straight in patt. until armholes measure 19 (20, 21) cm. (7½ (8, 8½) in.), ending with a wrong side row.

To shape neck *Next row:* Work 13 (16, 19), k. 2 tog., patt. 38 sts. and slip these 38 sts. on to a spare needle, k. 2 tog., patt. to end. Work each side separately. Dec. 1 st. at neck edge on next 6 rows. 8 (11, 14) sts. Cast off. Rejoin yarn to neck edge of rem. sts. and complete other side to match reversing shapings.

Right front
With 3¼ mm. needles, cast on 60 (66, 66) sts. and work 6 rows k. 1, p. 1 rib.
Buttonhole row: Rib 5, cast off 2, rib to end.
Next row: Rib to last 5 sts., cast on 2, rib to end.
Cont. in rib until 18 rows have been worked, inc. 2 sts. evenly along last rib row – 62 (68, 68) sts. Slip 12 sts. at inside edge on to a safety pin for front band – 50 (56, 56) sts. Work in patt. as for back to armhole, ending with a right side row.

To shape armhole Cast off 8 sts. at beg. of next row, then 5 sts. on foll. alt. row. Dec. 1 st. at same edge on foll. 5 alt. rows – 32 (38, 38) sts. Work straight until armhole measures 8 cm. (3 in.) ending at front edge.

To shape neck Cast off 12 sts. at beg. of next row then dec. 1 st. at neck edge on every row until 8 (11, 14) sts. remain. When work matches back to shoulder, cast off.

Left front
Work as for right front, omitting buttonholes and reversing shapings.

Left front band
Return to sts. of left front band and with 3¾ mm. needles, work in k. 1, p. 1 rib until band when slightly stretched fits left front edge. Leave sts. on a spare needle. Mark positions for buttons, the first 6 rows from lower edge and 4 more spaced evenly allowing for 6th button to be at beg. of neckband.

Right front band
Return to sts. of right front band and work to match left front band, making buttonholes to correspond with button positions as before. When correct length has been reached, leave sts. on a spare needle.

Neckband
Join shoulder seams. With 3¼ mm. needles, work buttonhole row over 12 sts. of right front band, pick up and k. 36 (40, 44) sts. along right front edge, 8 sts. across right back neck, work across 38 sts. of back neck in k. 1, p. 1 rib, pick up and k. 8 sts. along left back neck, 36 (40, 44) sts. along left front neck and work in k. 1, p. 1 rib across 12 sts. of left front band – 150 (158, 166) sts. Work in k. 1, p. 1 rib completing buttonhole as set. Work 4 more rows in rib, then cast off ribwise.

Armbands
With 3¼ mm. needles and right side facing, pick up and k. 98 (104, 110) sts. along right armhole edge. Work 5 rows in k. 1, p. 1 rib then cast off firmly ribwise. Work left armband to match.

TO MAKE UP

Join side seams and armhole bands. Stitch on front bands. Sew on buttons.

Slimline Tonic

MATERIALS

Rowan handknit DK cotton.
For cardigan: 14 (15, 16) 50 g. balls pink (D); one pair each 3¾ mm. (no. 9) and 4½ mm. (no. 7) knitting needles; a cable needle; 6 buttons; spare needles; 2 stitch holders.
For vest: 2 (3, 3) 50 g. balls cream (A); 1 (1, 1) 50 g. ball lilac (B); 1 (1, 1) 50 g. ball blue (C); 1 (1, 1) 50 g. ball pink (D); one pair of 4½ mm. (no. 7) knitting needles.

TENSION

19 stitches and 28 rows to 10 cm. (4 in.) measured over stocking stitch using 4½ mm. (no. 7) needles.

MEASUREMENTS

For cardigan:
To fit bust 86 (91, 97) cm., 34 (36, 38) in. (fitting loosely).
Actual measurement 98 (102, 106), 38 (40, 42) in.
Length from back neck 71 (72, 73), 28 (28½, 29) in.
Sleeve seam (all sizes) 44 cm., 17½ in.
For vest:
To fit bust 81 (86, 91) cm., 32 (34, 36) in. (fitting tightly).
Actual measurement 84 (88, 92) cm., 33 (34½, 36) in.
Length from shoulder 53 (54, 55) cm., 20¾ (21, 21½) in.

ABBREVIATIONS

alt., alternate; beg., begin(ning); cont., continue; C4B, slip the next 4 sts. on to a cable needle and hold at back of work, k. 4 sts. from left-hand needle, then k. 4 sts. from cable needle; C4F, slip the next 4 sts. on to a cable needle and hold at front of work, k. 4 sts. from left-hand needle, then k. 4 sts. from cable needle; dec., decreas(ing); foll., follow(ing); folls., follows; inc., increas(ing); k., knit; p., purl; patt., pattern; rem., remain(ing); rep., repeat; RS, right side; skpo, slip one, knit one, pass the slip stitch over;

st(s)., stitch(es); st. st., stocking stitch; tog., together; WS, wrong side.

Note Figures in brackets refer to the larger sizes. One set of figures refers to all sizes.

> A long cardigan, patterned with snaky cables, curves to the body and is matched with a broadly striped sleeveless cotton vest.

INSTRUCTIONS

CARDIGAN

Back
Cast on 96 (100, 104) sts. using 3¾ mm. needles. Work in k. 2, p. 2 rib for 8 cm. (3¼ in.) inc. 1 st. at each end of last row – 98 (102, 106) sts. Change to 4½ mm. needles and work in patt. as follows:
Row 1 (RS): K. 10 (12, 14) sts., * p. 2, k. 8, p. 2, k. 10, rep. from * to last 0 (2, 4) sts., k. 0 (2, 4).
Row 2 and every foll. alt. row: P. 10 (12, 14) sts., * k. 2, p. 8, k. 2, p. 10, rep. from * to last 0 (2, 4) sts., p. 0 (2, 4).
Rows 3 and 5: Work as for row 1.
Row 7: K. 10 (12, 14) sts., * p. 2, C4F, p. 2, k. 10, rep. from * to last 0 (2, 4) sts., k. 0 (2, 4).
Rows 9, 11, 13, 15 and 17: Work as for row 1.
Row 19: K. 10 (12, 14) sts., * p. 2, C4B, p. 2, k. 10, rep. from * to last 0 (2, 4) sts., k. 0 (2, 4).
Rows 21 and 23: Work as for row 1.
Row 24: Work as for row 2.
These 24 rows form the patt. and are repeated throughout. Cont. straight in patt. until back measures 50 cm. (19¾ in.) from cast-on edge ending with a WS row.

To shape armholes Keeping patt. correct, cast off 3 (4, 5) sts. at beg. of next 2 rows, then dec. 1 st. at each end of the foll. 3 alt. rows – 86 (88, 90) sts. Cont. straight in patt. until back measures 69

(70, 71) cm. (27¼ (27½, 28) in.) from cast-on edge, ending with a WS row.

To shape shoulders Cast off 11 (12, 13) sts. at beg. of next 2 rows, and 9 sts. at beg. of foll. 4 rows. Leave rem. 28 sts. on a spare needle for back neck.

Pocket linings (work 2)
Cast on 26 sts. using 4½ mm. needles. Starting with a k. row work 28 rows in st. st., ending with a WS row. Leave sts. on a spare needle.

Left front
Cast on 48 (48, 52) sts. using 3¾ mm. needles. Work in k. 2, p. 2 rib for 8 cm. (3¼ in.) inc. 1 st. at each end of last row, and on *2nd size only* inc. a further 2 sts. across row – 50 (52, 54) sts. Change to 4½ mm. needles, and work in patt. as follows:
Row 1 (RS): K. 10 (12, 14) sts., p. 2, k. 8, p. 2, k. 10, p. 2, k. 8, p. 2, k. 6.
This row places the patt. Cont. work patt. as for back until 28 patt. rows have been worked in all.

To place pocket lining *Next row (RS):* Patt. 7 (9, 11) sts., slip next 26 sts. on to a stitch holder and in place of these patt. across the 26 sts. of first pocket lining, patt. to end. Cont. in patt. as before until front measures 38 cm. (15 in.) from cast-on edge, ending with a RS row.

To shape front and armholes Keeping patt. correct, dec. 1 st. at beg. (neck edge) of next row, then at the same edge on every foll. 5th row, *at the same time* when front measures 50 cm. from cast-on edge, ending at side edge, begin to shape armhole whilst continuing to shape front edge. Cast off 3 (4, 5) sts. at beg. of next row, then dec. 1 st. at same edge on the foll. 3 alt. rows. Now, keeping armhole edge straight, cont. to shape front edge as before until 29 (30, 31) sts. rem., then cont. straight on these sts. until front matches back to shoulder shaping ending at armhole edge.

To shape shoulder Cast off 11 (12, 13) sts. at beg. of next row, then 9 sts. at beg. of foll. alt. row. Work 1 row, then cast off rem. 9 sts.

Right front

Cast on and work as for left front, but place pattern as follows:
Row 1 (RS): K. 6, p. 2, k. 8, p. 2, k. 10, p. 2, k. 8, p. 2, k. 10 (12, 14) sts.
This row places the patt. Cont. to work patt. as for back until 28 patt. rows have been worked in all.

To place pocket lining *Next row (RS):* Patt. 17 sts., slip next 26 sts. on to a stitch holder and in place of these patt. across the 26 sts. of second pocket lining, patt. to end. Complete to match left front, reversing all shapings.

Sleeves (make 2)

Cast on 44 (48, 48) sts. using 3¾ mm. needles. Work in k. 2, p. 2 rib for 8 cm. (3¼ in.) inc. 1 st. at each end of last row for *1st and 3rd sizes only* – 46 (48, 50) sts. Change to 4½ mm. needles and work in patt. as follows:
Row 1 (RS): K. 8 (9, 10) sts., p. 2, k. 8 *, p. 2, k. 6, p. 2, k. 8 *, p. 2, k. 8 (9, 10) sts.
This row places the patt. Cont. in patt. as now set working cable patt. over groups of sts. marked * only *at the same time* inc. 1 st. at each end of *every foll. 5th* row until there are 78 (80, 82) sts. on the needle, working inc. sts. into st. st. on either side. Cont. straight until sleeve measures 44 cm. (17¼ in.) from cast-on edge, ending with a WS row.

To shape top Keeping patt. correct, cast off 2 (3, 4) sts. at beg. of next 2 rows, then dec. 1 st. at each end of *every row* until 26 sts. remain on needle. Cast off 8 sts. at beg. of next 2 rows. Cast off rem. 10 sts.

Pocket edgings (alike)

With 3¾ mm. needles, slip the 26 sts. from one stitch holder on to left-hand needle and work in rib as folls.:
Row 1 (RS): P. 2, * k. 2, p. 2 rep. from * to end.
Row 2: K. 2, * p. 2, k. 2 rep. from * to end.
Rep. last 2 rows twice more. Cast off evenly in rib.

Front edging

Carefully join both shoulder seams matching cable patt. Mark points on both fronts where neck shaping begins with a coloured thread.

Right front edging With RS facing and 3¾ mm. needles, pick up and k. 68 sts. up to first marker, 50 (54, 58) sts. up to shoulder seam and 14 sts. to centre back neck – 132 (136, 140) sts. Work 5 rows in k. 2, p. 2 rib.

Buttonhole row (RS): Rib 8 sts., (yarn forward, k. 2 tog., rib 10 sts.) 5 times, yarn forward, k. 2 tog., rib to end (6 buttonholes worked). Work 4 more rows in rib. Cast off evenly in rib.

Left front edging Work left front edging to match right front edging, omitting buttonholes.

TO MAKE UP

Press all pieces (omitting ribbing) gently on WS using a warm iron over a damp cloth. Set in sleeves. Join side and sleeve seams. Stitch pocket linings in position on WS, pocket tops on RS. Join front edgings neatly at centre back. Sew on buttons.

VEST

INSTRUCTIONS

Back and front (both alike)

Cast on 79 (83, 87) sts. using 4½ mm. needles and yarn A. K. 3 rows to form border. Now, starting with a k. row, work 20 rows in st. st., ending with a WS row. Change to yarn B and work 22 rows in st. st. Change to yarn C and work 22 rows in st. st. Change to yarn D and work 22 rows in st. st. Change to yarn A (work in this colour from now on) and, starting with a k. row, work 3 rows in st. st.
Next row (WS): K. 9, p. 22 (24, 26) sts., k. 17, p. 22 (24, 26) sts., k. 9.
Next row (RS): K.
Rep. these 2 rows once more.

To shape armholes and neck *Next row (WS):* Cast off 6 sts. knitwise, k. 3, p. 22 (24, 26) sts., k. 3, cast off centre 11 sts. knitwise for neck, k. 3, p. 22 (24, 26) sts., k. 3, cast off rem. 6 sts. knitwise. With RS facing, rejoin yarn and cont. on first set of sts. only.
Row 1: K. 3, skpo, k. to last 5 sts., k. 2 tog., k. 3.
Row 2: K. 3, p. to last 3 sts., k. 3.
Rep. these 2 rows until 12 sts. rem. ending with a 2nd row.
Next row: K. 3, skpo, k. to end of row (11 sts.).
Working the 3 st. garter st. border as set, work 32 rows straight on these 11 sts. for straps. Cast off. With RS facing, rejoin yarn to rem. sts. and shape as folls.:
Row 1: K. 3, skpo, k. to last 5 sts., k. 2 tog., k. 3.
Row 2: K. 3, p. to last 3 sts., k. 3.
Rep. these 2 rows until 12 sts. rem. ending with a 2nd row.
Next row: K. to last 5 sts., k. 2 tog., k. 3 (11 sts.).
Now complete strap to match first strap.

TO MAKE UP

Press both pieces gently on WS using a warm iron over a damp cloth. Join strap seams and side seams matching stripes. Press seams.

Rib

MATERIALS

5 (6, 6, 7) 100 g. balls Twilleys Pegasus; 10 (11, 12, 13) 50 g. balls Twilleys Dishcloth Cotton, C22; a pair each 9 mm. (no. 00) and 10 mm. (no. 000) knitting needles. Spare needle. Stitch holder.

TENSION

8 stitches and 13 rows to 10 cm. (4 in.) over stocking stitch, using 10 mm. (no. 000) needles, and 1 strand of each yarn together.

MEASUREMENTS

To fit bust 92 (97, 102, 107) cm., 36 (38, 40, 42) in., fitting loosely.
Length from shoulder 60 cm., 23½ in.
Sleeve seam (all sizes) 50 cm., 19¾ in.

ABBREVIATIONS

beg., beginning; dec., decrease; foll., following; inc., increase; k., knit; p., purl; patt., pattern; rep., repeat; RS, right side; st(s)., stitch(es); tog., together; WS, wrong side.

INSTRUCTIONS

Note One strand of each yarn is knitted together throughout.

Back
With 9 mm. needles, using one strand of each yarn tog., cast on 51 (53, 55, 57) sts. Work in k. 1, p. 1 rib for 4 rows.
Inc. row: Rib 4 (5, 6, 7), * inc. in next st., rib 6, rep. from * 5 times more, inc. in next st. rib 4 (5, 6, 7) sts. – 58 (60, 62, 64) sts. Change to 10 mm. needles and work in patt. as follows:
Row 1 (RS): P. 10 (2, 3, 4), * k. 2, p. 7, rep. from * to last 12 (4, 5, 6) sts., p. 10 (2, 3, 4).
Row 2: K. 10 (2, 3, 4), * slip 2 purlwise with yarn at front, k. 7, rep. from * to last

Quickly knitted man's sweater in cotton and dishcloth cotton.
Very easy.

12 (4, 5, 6) sts., slip 2 purlwise with yarn at front, k. 10 (2, 3, 4).
These 2 rows form the patt. and are repeated throughout. Cont. straight in patt. until back measures 58 cm. (23 in.) from cast-on edge, ending with a WS row.

To shape shoulders Cast off 16 (17, 18, 19) sts. at beg. of next 2 rows. Leave rem. 26 sts. on a spare needle for back neck.

Front
Work as for back until 6 fewer rows than on back to shoulder have been worked.

To shape front neck Next row: Patt. 19 (20, 21, 22) sts. turn: and work on these sts. only.
** Dec. 1 st. at neck edge on every row until 16 (17, 18, 19) sts. remain. Work a few rows straight until front measures same as back to shoulder, ending at side edge. Cast off. Return to rem. sts. and slip centre 20 sts. on to a stitch holder, with RS facing rejoin yarn to neck edge of rem. 19 (20, 21, 22) sts. and patt. to end of row. Patt. 1 row. Now work as for first side from ** to end.

Sleeves (make 2)
With 9 mm. needles, using one strand of each yarn tog., cast on 25 (25, 29, 29) sts. Work in k. 1, p. 1 rib for 6 rows.
Inc. row: Rib 1 (1, 3, 3) * inc. in next st. rib 2, rep. from * 6 times more, inc. in next st., rib 2 (2, 4, 4) – 33 (33, 37, 37) sts.). Change to 10 mm. needles, and work in pattern as follows:
Row 1 (RS): P. 2 (2, 4, 4), * k. 2, p. 7, rep. from * to last 4 (4, 6, 6) sts., k. 2, p. 2 (2, 4, 4). This row sets the patt. Cont. in patt. as for back, *at the same time*, inc. 1 st. at each end of every foll. 6th row until there are 51 (51, 55, 55) sts. on the needle, working inc. sts. into the patt. Work 4 more rows straight then cast off loosely.

Collar
Join right shoulder seam. With RS facing, using one strand of each yarn tog., and 9 mm. needle pick up and k. 6 (6, 7, 7) sts. down left front neck edge, k. across the 20 sts. of front neck, pick up and k. 6 (6, 7, 7) sts. up right front neck, then k. across the 26 sts. of back neck – 58 (58, 60, 60) sts. Work in k. 1, p. 1 rib for 15 rows. Cast off loosely ribwise.

TO MAKE UP

Join left shoulder seam and collar seam. With centre of cast-off edges of sleeves to shoulder seams, sew sleeves in position. Join sleeve seams and side seams. Roll collar over on to right side.

Cowl

MATERIALS

6 (6, 7) 50 g. balls Hayfield Raw Cotton; 5 (6, 6) 50 g. balls Hayfield Grampian Chunky; a pair 10 mm. (no. 000) knitting needles; spare needle; stitch holder.

TENSION

8 stitches and 16 rows to 10 cm. (4 in.) over garter stitch using 10 mm. (no. 000) needles and two strands of cotton and one strand of wool together.

MEASUREMENTS

To fit bust 66 (71, 76) cm., 26 (28, 30) in., fitting loosely.
Actual measurement 87.5 (92.5, 97.5) cm., 34½ (36½, 38¼ in.).
Length from shoulder 38 (40, 42) cm., 14 (14.5, 15) in.
Sleeve seam (all sizes) 36 (37, 38) cm., 14 (14½, 15) in. (when not rolled back).

ABBREVIATIONS

beg., beginning; cont., continue; dec., decrease; foll., following; g. st., garter stitch – every row knit; inc., increase; k., knit; p., purl; rem., remaining; st(s)., stitch(es); tog., together.

INSTRUCTIONS

Note Two strands of cotton are used with one strand of wool throughout.

Back

Using two strands of cotton and one strand of wool tog., with 10 mm. needles, cast on 35 (37, 39) sts. Cont. straight in g. st. (every row knit), until work measures 19 (20, 21) cm. from beg.

To shape armholes Cast off 4 sts. at beg. of next 2 rows – 27 (29, 31) sts. ** K. 28 (30, 32) more rows.

To shape shoulders Cast off 6 sts. at

This cute top for a little girl is warm and practical as well with a cowl hood you can pull right up.
Very easy.

beg. of next 2 rows. Leave rem. 15 (17, 19) sts. on a spare needle for back neck.

Front

Work as for back to **. K. 22 (24, 26) more rows.

To shape front neck Next row: K. 10 (11, 11) sts. turn: and work on this set of sts. only. *** Dec. 1 st. at neck edge on next 4 (5, 5) rows. Work 1 (0, 0) row straight. Cast off rem. 6 sts. Return to rem. sts. and slip centre 7 (7, 9) sts. on to a stitch holder. Rejoin yarn to neck edge of rem. 10 (11, 11) sts. and k. to end of row. K. 1 row. Now work as for first side from *** to end.

Sleeves (make 2)

Using two strands of cotton and one strand of wool tog., with 10 mm. needles, cast on 20 (22, 24) sts. K. 9 rows. Cont. to work in g. st., but inc. 1 st. at each end of next row and every foll. 8th row until 30 (32, 34) sts. are on the needle. Now cont. straight in g. st. until sleeve measures 41 (42, 43) cm. (15¾ (16½, 17) in.) from beg. Cast off fairly loosely.

Cowl hood

Join right shoulder seam. Using two strands of cotton and one strand of wool, with 10 mm. needles and RS facing, pick up and k. 8 (9, 10) sts. along left front neck edge, k. across the 7 (7, 9) sts. of front neck, pick up and k. 8 (9, 10) sts. along right front neck edge, then k. across the 15 (17, 19) sts. of back neck – 38 (42, 48) sts. Work straight in g. st. for 30 (32, 34) cm. (11¾ (12½, 13¼) in.). Cast off loosely.

TO MAKE UP

Join left shoulder seam, and seam of cowl hood. With centre of sleeves to shoulder seams, sew cast-off edges to straight edges of armholes, and join the top 5 cm. (2 in.) of sleeves to cast-off groups of 4 sts. at armholes. Join side seams and sleeve seams. Turn over cuffs and cowl neck as required.

Big Cables

MATERIALS

6 (6) 100 g. balls Twilleys Capricorn Bulky; 7 (8) 50 g. balls Twilleys Angelspun; 8 (9) 40 g. balls Twilleys Candy Cotton; a pair each 10 mm. (no. 000) and 8 mm. (no. 0) knitting needles; a cable needle; spare needle.

TENSION

8 stitches and 13 rows to 10 cm. (4 in.) over stocking stitch using 10 mm. (no. 000) needles and one strand of each yarn together.

MEASUREMENTS

To fit bust 81–86 (92–97) cm., 32–34 (36–38) in. (fitting loosely).
Length from shoulder 65 (68) cm., 25½ (26¾) in.
Sleeve (all sizes) 48 cm., 19 in.

ABBREVIATIONS

beg., beginning; C4F, slip next 4 sts. on to cable needle and hold at front of work, k. 4, then k. 4 from cable needle; dec., decrease; foll., following; inc., increase; k., knit; p., purl; patt., pattern; rem., remaining; rep., repeat; st. st., stocking stitch; st(s)., stitch(es); tog., together.

INSTRUCTIONS

Note One strand of each yarn is used together throughout.

Back

With 8 mm. needles, and using one strand of each of the three yarns tog., cast on 56 (62) sts. Work in k. 1, p. 1 rib for 7 rows. Change to 10 mm. needles and work in patt. as follows:
Row 1 (RS): P. 9 (12), * k. 8, p. 7, rep. from * to last 17 (20) sts., k. 8, p. 9 (12).
Row 2: K. 9 (12), * p. 8, k. 7, rep. from * to last 17 (20) sts., p. 8, k. 9 (12).
Rep. rows 1 and 2 twice more.

The subtle mixture of cream yarns makes an elegant tunic in a strong shape with big cables, worked on extra large needles.
Very easy.

Row 7: P. 9 (12), * C4F, p. 7, rep. from * to last 17 (20) sts., C4F, p. 9 (12).
Row 8: As row 2.
Rows 9 and 10: As rows 1 and 2.
These 10 rows form the patt. When patt. has been worked 7 (8) times in all, then work rows 1–8 (1–2) once more, thus ending with a WS row.

To shape shoulders Cast off 17 (19) sts. at beg. of next 2 rows. Leave rem. 22 (24) sts. on a spare needle for back neck.

Front

Work as for back until 74 (78) patt. rows in all have been worked, thus ending with a WS row.

To shape front neck *Next row:* Patt. 19 (21) sts., p. 2 tog., turn; work on these sts. only. ** Dec. 1 st. at neck edge on the next 3 rows. Cast off rem. 17 (19) sts. Return to rem. sts., with RS facing, and cast off centre 14 (16) sts., p. 2 tog., patt. to end of row, and work 1 row on these 20 (22) sts. Now work as for first side from ** to end.

Sleeves (make 2)

With 8 mm. needles and using one strand of each of the 3 yarns tog., cast on 26 (30) sts. Work in k. 1, p. 1 rib for 6 rows.
Inc. row: Rib 0 (2) * inc. in next st., rib 3, rep. from * 5 times more, inc. in next st., rib 1 (3) – 33 (37) sts.
Change to 10 mm. needles and work in pattern as follows:
Row 1 (RS): P. 5 (7), k. 8, p. 7, k. 8, p. 5 (7).
This row sets the patt. Cont. to work cables as set for back, *at the same time*, inc. 1 st. at each end of the 7th row and then every foll. 6th row until there are 47 (51) sts. on the needle, working inc. sts. into reverse st. st. Cont. straight in patt. until sleeve measures 48 cm. from cast-on-edge. Cast off loosely.

Cowl collar

With 10 mm. needles, using one strand of each of the 3 yarns tog., cast on 50 (54) sts. Starting with a k. row, cont. straight in st. st. for 24 cm. (9¼ in.). Cast off loosely.

TO MAKE UP

Join shoulder seams *on the right side* with backstitch to form ridge. With centre of cast-off edges of sleeves to shoulder seams, sew sleeves in position on *the right side* with a backstitch, to a depth of 26 (28) cm. (10¼ (11) in.) down on both back and front from shoulder. Join sleeve seams and side seams on the wrong side. With p. sides together, join collar seam. With right sides together and collar seam to left shoulder seam, sew on collar. Turn over to required depth.

Squares

64

MATERIALS

11 (12, 12) 50 g. balls Sirdar Country Style Chunky or 13 (14, 14) 50 g. balls W. H. Smith Pure Wool Chunky; a pair each 8 mm. (no. 0) and 10 mm. (no. 000) knitting needles; 2 spare needles.

TENSION

9 stitches and 13 rows to 10 cm. (4 in.) over pattern with yarn used double on 10 mm. (no. 000) needles.

MEASUREMENTS

To fit bust 76 (82, 87) cm., 30 (32, 34) in., fitting loosely.
Actual measurement 93 (97.5, 102) cm., 36½ (38, 40) in.
Length from shoulder 40 (43, 46) cm., 15¾ (17, 18) in.
Sleeve seam (all sizes) 38 (39, 41) cm., 15 (15½, 16½) in. (when not rolled back).

ABBREVIATIONS

alt., alternate; beg., beginning; cont., continue; dec., decrease; foll., following; inc., increase; k., knit; p., purl; patt., pattern; rem., remaining; RS, right side; st(s)., stitch(es); WS, wrong side.

INSTRUCTIONS

Note Yarn is used double throughout.

Back
With 8 mm. needles and yarn used double, cast on 41 (43, 45) sts. Work in k. 1, p. 1 rib for 5 rows, working an inc. at end of last rib row – 42 (44, 46) sts. Change to 10 mm. needles and work in patt. as follows:
Row 1 (RS): K. 3 (0, 5), * p. 4, k. 4, rep. from * to last 7 (4, 9) sts., p. 4, k. 3 (0, 5).
Row 2: P. 3 (0, 5), * k. 4, p. 4, rep. from * to last 7 (4, 9) sts., k. 4, p. 3 (0, 5).
Row 3: As row 1.
Row 4: As row 2.
Row 5: As row 2.

Cream yarn used double is quickly knitted in a squares pattern to make a smart jumper for a little boy.
Very easy.

Row 6: As row 1.
Rows 7–8: Rep. rows 5 and 6.
These 8 rows form the patt. Work the 8 patt. rows 5 (5, 6) times more, then rows 1 to 4 *for 2nd size only*, thus ending with a WS row.

To shape shoulders Cast off 13 sts. at beg. of next 2 rows. Leave rem. 16 (18, 20) sts. on a spare needle for back neck.

Front
Work as for back until 6 (8, 8) fewer rows have been worked than on back to shoulder.

To shape front neck *Next row (RS facing):* Patt. 17 sts., turn: work on these sts. only. ** Dec. 1 st. at neck edge on next 4 rows – 13 sts. Patt. 1 (3, 3) row(s)

straight. Cast off. Return to rem. sts. and slip centre 8 (10, 12) sts. on to a spare needle, with RS facing rejoin yarn to neck edge of rem. 17 sts., and patt. to end of row. Patt. 1 row. Now work as for first side from ** to end.

Sleeves (make 2)
With 8 mm. needles and yarn used double, cast on 21 (23, 25) sts. Work in k. 1, p. 1 rib for 7 rows, working an inc. at end of last rib row – 22 (24, 26) sts. Change to 10 mm. needles, and work in patt. as follows:
Row 1 (RS): P. 1 (2, 3), * k. 4, p. 4 rep. from * to last 5 (6, 7) sts., k. 4, p. 1 (2, 3). This row sets the patt. Cont. in patt. as for back, *at the same time* inc. 1 st. at each end of *every* foll. 6th row until there are 36 (38, 40) sts. on the needle, working inc. sts. into the patt. Patt. 1 (3, 5) row(s) straight. Cast off loosely.

Neckband
Join right shoulder seam. With RS facing, using yarn double, with 8 mm. needles, pick up and k. 7 (8, 8) sts. down left front neck, k. across the 8 (10, 12) centre front sts., pick up and k. 7 (8, 8) sts. up right front neck, k. across the 16 (18, 20) back neck sts. – 38 (44, 48) sts. Work in k. 1, p. 1 rib for 5 rows. Cast off loosely ribwise.

TO MAKE UP

Join left shoulder seam and neckband. With centre of cast-off edges of sleeves to shoulder seams, sew sleeves in position. Join sleeve seams and side seams. Turn over cuffs as required.

Blue Moon

MATERIALS

21 (22) 50 g. balls Sunbeam Aran Knit in pale blue (no. 10) or 27 (28) 50 g. balls W. H. Smith Pure Wool Chunky; a pair each 4½ mm. (no. 7) and 5 mm. (no. 6) knitting needles; a cable needle; a 4½ mm. circular needle.

TENSION

16 stitches and 20 rows to 10 cm. (4 in.) over st. st. using 5 mm. (no. 6) needles.

MEASUREMENTS

To fit bust 81–86 (91–97) cm., 32–34 (36–38) in.
Length 68 (70) cm., 26¾ (27½) in.
Sleeve seam (both sizes) 45 cm., 17¾ in.

ABBREVIATIONS

B.Cr., back cross, by slipping next st. on to cable needle and holding at back of work, k. 2 then p. 1 from cable needle; beg., beginning; C4B, slip the next 2 sts. on to cable needle, and hold at back of work, k. 2, then k. 2 from cable needle; C4BP, slip next 2 sts. on to cable needle and hold at back of work, k. 2, then p. 2 sts. from cable needle; C4F, slip next 2 sts. on to cable needle and hold at front of work, k. 2, then k. 2 sts. from cable needle; C4FP, slip next 2 sts. on to cable needle and hold at front of work, p. 2 then k. 2 sts. from cable needle; cont., continue; dec., decrease; F.Cr., slip next 2 sts. on to cable needle and hold at front of work, p. 1 then k. 2 from cable needle; foll., following; inc., increase; k., knit; p., purl; patt., pattern; rem., remaining; rep., repeat; RS, right side; sep., separately; st(s)., stitch(es); TBL, through back loop; WS, wrong side.

TRIPLE CABLE PATTERN

Worked over 26 sts.
Rows 1 and 3 (WS): K. 11, p. 4, k. 11.

Pure new wool sweater with extra deep V-neck, huge ornate twisted cabling and side seam slits.

Row 2: P. 11, C4B, p. 11.
Row 4: P. 9, C4B, C4F, p. 9.
Row 5 and every foll. alt. row: K. the k. sts. and p. the p. sts. as they face you.
Row 6: P. 7, C4BP, C4F, C4FP, p. 7.
Row 8: P. 5, C4BP, p. 2, k. 4, p. 2, C4FP, p. 5.
Row 10: P. 4, B.Cr., p. 4, C4F, p. 4, F.Cr., p. 4.
Row 12: P. 3, B.Cr., p. 3, C4B., C4F, p. 3, F.Cr., p. 3.
Row 14: P. 2, B.Cr., p. 2, C4BP, k. 4, C4FP, p. 2, F.Cr., p. 2.
Row 16: P. 2, k. 2, p. 1, C4BP, p. 2, C4B, p. 2, C4FP, p. 1, k. 2, p. 2.
Row 18: P. 2, k. 2, p. 1, k. 2, p. 4, k. 4, p. 4, k. 2, p. 1, k. 2, p. 2.
Row 20: P. 2, k. 2, p. 1, C4FP, p. 2, C4B, p. 2, C4BP, p. 1, k. 2, p. 2.
Row 22: P. 2, F.Cr., p. 2, C4FP, k. 4, C4BP, p. 2, B.Cr., p. 2.
Row 24: P. 3, F.Cr., p. 3, C4FP, C4BP, p. 3, B.Cr., p. 3.
Row 26: P. 4, F.Cr., p. 4, C4F, p. 4, B.Cr., p. 4.
Row 28: P. 5, C4FP, p. 2, k. 4, p. 2, C4BP, p. 5.
Row 30: P. 7, C4FP, C4F, C4BP, p. 7.
Row 32: P. 9, C4FP, C4BP, p. 9.
These 32 rows form patt.

Blue Moon

INSTRUCTIONS

Back
With 4½ mm. needles, cast on 124 (140) sts.

Row 1 rib (RS): K. 3, *p. 2, k. 2, rep. from * to last st., k. 1.

Row 2 rib: P. 3, *k. 2, p. 2, rep. from * to last st., p. 1.

Rep. these 2 rows until work measures 11 cm. (4¼ in.) from beg., ending with a row 2.

Inc. row: Rib 5 (3), * inc. in next st., rib 5 (6), rep. from * to last 5 (4) sts., inc. in next st., rib 4 (3) – 144 (160) sts. Change to 5 mm. needles.

Cont. in patt.:

Row 1 (WS): K. 5 (p. 2, k. 6) 2 (3) times, p. 2, k. 3, work 1st row of cable panel over next 26 sts., k. 3, (p. 2, k. 6) 4 times, p. 2, k. 3, work 1st row of cable panel over next 26 sts., k. 3 (p. 2, k. 6) 2 (3) times, p. 2, k. 5.

Row 2: P. 5, (k. 2, p. 6) 2 (3) times, k. 2, p. 3, work 2nd row of cable panel over next 26 sts., p. 3 (k. 2, p. 6) 4 times, k. 2, p. 3, work 2nd row of cable panel over next 26 sts., p. 3 (k. 2, p. 6) 2 (3) times, k. 2, p. 5.

Rows 3 to 32: Rep. 1st and 2nd rows but working rows 3 to 32 of cable panel. These 32 rows form patt. **.

Rep. rows 1 to 32 twice, then row 1 to 29 again.

To shape shoulders Cast off 23 (27) sts. at beg. of next 2 rows and 24 (28) sts. on the foll. 2 rows. Leave rem. 50 sts. on a spare needle.

Front
Work as back to **. Rep. rows 1 to 15.

To shape neck *Row 1:* Patt. 71 (79) sts., turn. Cont. on these sts. only and leave rem. sts. on a spare needle. Keeping patt. correct, dec. 1 st at neck edge on next row and every foll. 3rd row until 47 (55) sts. rem. Cont. straight until front matches back to shoulder, thus ending with row 29.

To shape shoulders Cast off 23 (27) sts. at beg. of next row. Work 1 row. Cast off rem. 24 (28) sts.

With RS facing, sl. centre 2 sts. on to a safety pin, rejoin yarn to inner end of rem. 71 (79) sts. and patt. to end. Complete to match first side.

Sleeves
With 4½ mm. needles, cast on 50 (54) sts. Work 6 cm. (2½ in.) in k. 2, p. 2 rib, beg. WS rows p. 2 and ending with a RS row.

Inc. row: Inc. in first st., * inc. in next st., rib 1, rep. from * to last st., inc. in last st. – 76 (82) sts.

Change to 5 mm. needles.

Cont. in patt.:

Row 1 (RS): P. 5 (0), * k. 2, p. 6, rep. from * to last 7 (2) sts., k. 2, p. 5 (0).

Row 2: K. 5 (0), * p. 2, k. 6, rep. from * to last 7 (2) sts., p. 2, k. 5 (0).

These two rows form patt. Cont. in patt. inc. 1 st. at each end of next row and every foll. 7th row until there are 100 (106) sts., working inc. sts. into patt. Patt. straight until sleeve measures 45 cm. (17¾ in.) from cast-on edge. Cast off loosely.

Neckband
Join shoulder seams. With RS facing and using 4½ mm. circular needle, work in k. 2, p. 2 rib across 50 sts. of back neck, pick up and k. 62 sts. down left front neck, k. across 2 sts. on safety pin then pick up and k. 62 sts. up right front neck – 176 sts.

Mark the 2 sts. at centre front with a coloured thread.

Next round: Work in k. 2, p. 2 rib to within 2 sts. of marked sts., rib 2 tog., k. 2, rib 2 tog. TBL, work in k. 2, p. 2 rib to end of round. Rep. last round 15 times. Cast off in rib. dec. as before at either side of marked sts.

TO MAKE UP

Press garment lightly if required. Place markers on side edges of back and front 26 (27) cm. (10¼ (10½) in.) from shoulder seams. Sew on sleeves between markers. Leaving rib open join side seams. Join sleeve seams.

Geometric

MATERIALS

17 (18, 19) 50 g. balls Pingouin Iceberg, or 16 (17, 18) 50 g. balls Pingouin Typhon; a pair each 5½ mm. (no. 5) and 6 mm. (no. 4) knitting needles; 6 buttons.

TENSION

12 stitches and 16 rows to 10 cm. (4 in.) over stocking stitch using 6 mm. (no. 4) needles.

MEASUREMENTS

To fit bust 86 (91, 97) cm., 34 (36, 38) in.
Length 54 (55, 56) cm., 21¼ (21¾, 22) in.
Sleeve seam (all sizes) 43 cm., 17 in.

ABBREVIATIONS

beg., beginning; cont., continue; dec., decrease; foll., following; inc., increase; k., knit; p., purl; patt., pattern; rep., repeat; rev. st. st., reverse stocking stitch; st(s)., stitch(es); st. st., stocking stitch; tog., together.

INSTRUCTIONS

Back

Using 5½ mm. needles, cast on 77 (81, 85) sts. Work in k. 1, p. 1 rib for 6 cm. (2½ in.), inc. 1 st. at end of last rib row – 78 (82, 86) sts. Change to 6 mm. needles and work in patt. as folls.
Row 1: K. 39 (41, 43), p. 39 (41, 43).
Row 2: As row 1.
These 2 rows form patt. Cont. in patt. until back measures 52 (53, 54) cm. (20½ (21, 21¼) in.) from beg.

To shape neck Work 28 (30, 32), k. 2 tog., turn and cont. on this group of sts. Dec. 1 st. at neck edge on next 3 rows – 26 (28, 30) sts. Cast off. Slip centre 18 sts. on to a spare needle. Rejoin yarn to rem. group of sts. at neck edge and complete to match first group.

Right front

Using 5½ mm. needles, cast on 37 (39, 41) sts. Work in k. 1, p. 1 rib for 6 cm. (2½ in.) **. Change to 6 mm. needles and work in patt. as folls.
Row 1: 1st and 2nd sizes: P. 6, * k. 1, p. 5; rep. from * to last 1 (3) sts., p. 1 (3).
3rd size: P. 6, * k. 1, p. 5; rep. from * to last 5 sts., k. 1, p. 4.
Row 2: 1st and 2nd sizes: K. 1 (3), * k. 5, p. 1; rep. from * to last 6 sts., k. 6.
3rd size: K. 4, p. 1, * k. 5, p. 1; rep. from * to last 6 sts., k. 6.
These 2 rows form patt. Cont. in patt. until work measures 47 (48, 49) cm. (18½ (19, 19¼) in.) from beg., ending with a 2nd row.

To shape neck *Next row:* Cast off 9 sts., work to end. Dec. 1 st. at neck edge on next 2 rows – 26 (28, 30) sts. Cont. on these sts. until work measures same as back. Cast off.

Left front

Work as right front to **. Change to 6 mm. needles and work in patt. as folls. Work 6 rows in st. st. beg. with a k. row.
Next 2 rows: P.
These 8 rows form patt. Cont. in patt. until work measures 47 (48, 49) cm. (18½ (19, 19¼) in.) from beg. ending with a right side row.

To shape neck *Next row:* Cast off 9 sts., work to end. Dec. 1 st. at neck edge on next 2 rows – 26 (28, 30) sts. Cont. on these sts. until work measures same as back. Cast off.

Right sleeve

Using 5½ mm. needles cast on 35 (39, 43) sts. Work in k. 1, p. 1 rib for 7 cm. (2¾ in.). Change to 6 mm. needles and work in st. st. inc. 1 st. at each end of next and every foll. 4th row until there are 69 (73, 77) sts. Cast off.

Left sleeve Work as right sleeve, but work in rev. st. st.

Right front band

Using 5½ mm. needles, cast on 10 sts. and work 6 rows in k. 1, p. 1 rib.
Buttonhole row: Rib 4, cast off 2, rib to end.
Next row: Rib 4, cast on 2, rib to end.
Work 12 rows more in rib. Cont. to work buttonholes as before, 12 rows apart, until 5th buttonhole has been worked. Work 10 rows more in rib. Leave sts. on a safety pin.

Left front band

Work as right front band omitting buttonholes.

Neckband

Using 5½ mm. needles, rib across the 10 sts. of right front band, pick up and k. 14 sts. along right front neck edge, 6 sts. across right back neck, k. across the 18 sts. of back neck, pick up and k. 6 sts. along left back neck, 14 sts. along left front neck, then work in rib over the 10 sts. of left front band. Rib 1 row. Now work a buttonhole as before on next 2 rows. Rib 4 rows more. Cast off in rib.

TO MAKE UP

Join shoulder seams. Place markers for armholes 28 (29, 30) cm. (11 (11½, 11¾) in.) down from shoulders at side edges. Join sleeve and side seams to markers. Sew in sleeves. Stitch on front bands. Sew on buttons.

Long Shot

8 (9, 9) 50 g. balls Pingouin Vrille; a pair each 4 mm. (no. 8) and 4½ mm. (no. 7) knitting needles; 6 buttons.

TENSION

17 stitches and 21 rows to 10 cm. (4 in.) using 4½ mm. (no. 7) knitting needles.

MEASUREMENTS

To fit bust 86 (91, 97) cm., 34 (36, 38) in. Length 81 (82, 83) cm., 32 (32½, 33) in.

ABBREVIATIONS

alt., alternate; beg., beginning; cont., continue; dec., decrease; foll., following; k., knit; p., purl; patt., pattern; rem., remain(ing); rep., repeat; st(s)., stitch(es); tog., together.

INSTRUCTIONS

Back

With 4 mm. needles, cast on 90 (94, 98) sts. and work in k. 1, p. 1 rib for 8 cm. (3¼ in.). Change to 4½ mm. needles and work in stocking stitch until back measures 58 cm. (23 in.) from beg., ending with a p. row.

To shape armholes Cast off 6 sts. at beg. of next 2 rows. Dec. 1 st. at each end of next and every foll. alt. row until 72 (76, 80) sts. rem. Cont. straight until armhole measures 22 (23, 24) cm., (8¾ (9, 9½) in.) ending with a p. row.

To shape shoulders Cast off 7 (8, 9) sts. at beg. of next 4 rows, then 4 sts. at beg. of next 2 rows. Cast off rem. 36 sts.

Left front

With 4 mm. needles, cast on 44 (46, 48) sts. and work in k. 1, p. 1 rib for 8 cm. (3¼ in.), inc. 1 st. at end of last row – 45 (47, 49) sts.
Change to 4½ mm. needles and work in stocking stitch until work measures 56

A long tweedy waistcoat adds dash to a printed shirt and keeps the cold out.
Very easy.

cm. (22 in.) from beg., ending with a p. row.

To shape neck Cast off 1 st. at neck edge on next and every foll. 3rd row. Cont. straight until work measures 58 cm. (23 in.) from beg.

To shape armhole Cont. to dec. at neck edge and at the same time cast off 6 sts. at armhole edge, then dec. 1 st. at armhole on the foll. 3 alt. rows. Keeping armhole edge straight, cont. to dec. at neck edge on every foll. 3rd row until 18 (20, 22) sts. rem.
Cont. straight until front matches back to shoulder.

To shape shoulder Beg. at armhole edge, cast off 7 (8, 9) sts. on next and foll. alt. row, then cast off rem. 4 sts.

Right front

Work as for left front, reversing all shapings.

Front band

With 4 mm. needles, cast on 11 sts. and work 6 rows in k. 1, p. 1 rib.
Buttonhole row: Rib 4, cast off 2, rib to end.
Next row: Rib 5, cast on 2, rib to end.
Work 5 more buttonholes, each spaced 18 rows apart. Now cont. in rib without buttonholes, until band, when slightly stretched, fits up right front, across back neck and down left front. Cast off ribwise.

Armbands

Join shoulder seams. With right side facing and using 4 mm. needles, pick up and k. 94 (98, 102) sts. along right armhole edge. Work in k. 1, p. 1 rib for 7 rows, then cast off ribwise.
Work other armband to match.

Patch pockets

With 4 mm. needles, cast on 27 sts. and work in stocking stitch for 12 cm. (4¾ in.). Now work in k. 1, p. 1 rib for 5 cm. (2 in.) beg. first row with p. 1.
Cast off ribwise.

TO MAKE UP

Join side seams and armbands. Stitch patch pockets to fronts. Stitch front band in position. Sew on buttons.

Cherokee

MATERIALS

9 (10) 100 g. hanks Rowan Chunky Tweed in main colour (Indian Red 711), 2 (3) 100 g. hanks in contrast colour (warm orange 710); a pair each 6 mm. (no. 4) and 7 mm. (no. 2) knitting needles; 4 buttons; a cable needle; 2 spare needles, 2 stitch holders.

TENSION

12 stitches and 15 rows to 10 cm. (4 in.) measured over stocking stitch using 7 mm. (no. 2) needles.

MEASUREMENTS

To fit bust 81–86 (91–96 cm.), 32–34 (36–38) in. (fitting loosely).
Length from back neck 74 cm., 29 in.
Sleeve seam (all sizes) 46 cm., 18 in.

ABBREVIATIONS

alt., alternate; B.Cr., slip next st. on to cable needle and hold at back of work, k. 2 yarn C from left-hand needle, p. 1 yarn M from cable needle; beg., beginning; C., contrast shade; C4F, slip next 2 sts. on to cable needle and hold at front of work, k. 2 from left-hand needle, then k. 2 from cable needle; cont., continue; dec., decreas(ing); F.Cr., slip next 2 sts. on to cable needle and hold at front of work, p. 1 yarn M from left-hand needle then k. 2 yarn C from cable needle; foll., following; folls., follows; inc., increas(ing); k. knit; M., main shade; p., purl; patt., pattern; rem., remain(ing); rep., repeat; RS, right side; st(s)., stitch(es); st. st., stocking stitch; tog., together; WS, wrong side.

Note When working the fair isle and Aran patts. strand yarn not in use loosely across back of work over not more than 3 sts. at a time, spreading sts. to their correct width to ensure that fabric is kept elastic. Weave-in yarns if they are to be carried across more than 3 sts.

INSTRUCTIONS

Back
Cast on 80 (84) sts. using 6 mm. needles and M. Work 11 rows in k. 2, p. 2 rib, *on 2nd size only*, inc. 2 sts. evenly across last row – 80 (86) sts. Change to 7 mm. needles and work in patt. as folls., which is worked in st. st. beg. with a k. row unless otherwise stated, so only the colour details are given.
Rows 1–10: M.
Rows 11–16: Joining in C and work in st. st. across *chart A*, working between appropriate lines for size required.
Rows 17–24: M.
Rows 25–26: C.
Joining in M, work the 2-colour Aran diamond and moss st. patt. as folls.:
Row 27 (RS facing): K. 12 (15) M, C4F C, k. 10 M, C4F C, k. 20 M, C4F C, k. 10 M, C4F C, k. 12 (15) M.
Row 28: (and every foll. alt. row) K. all p. sts. of previous row, p. all k. sts. of previous row.
Row 29: K. 11 (14) M, *B.Cr., F.Cr., k. 8 M, B.Cr., F.Cr. *, k. 18 M, rep. from * to *, k. 11 (14) M.
Row 31: K. 10 (13) M, *B.Cr., k. 1 M, p. 1 M, F.Cr., k. 6 M, B.Cr., k. 1 M, p. 1 M, F.Cr. *, k. 16 M, rep. from * to *, k. 10 (13) M.
Row 33: K. 9 (12) M, *B.Cr., (k. 1 M, p. 1 M) twice, F.Cr., k. 4 M, B.Cr., (k. 1 M, p. 1 M) twice, F.Cr. *, k. 14 M, rep. from * to *, k. 9 (12) M.
Row 35: K. 8 (11) M, *B.Cr., (k. 1 M, p. 1 M) 3 times, F.Cr., k. 2 M, B.Cr., (k. 1 M, p. 1 M) 3 times, F.Cr. *, k. 12 M, rep. from * to *, k. 8 (11) M.
Row 37: K. 7 (10) M, *B.Cr., (k, 1 M, p. 1 M) 4 times, F.Cr., B.Cr., (k. 1 M, p. 1 M) 4 times, F.Cr. *, k. 10 M, rep. from * to *, k. 7 (10) M.
Row 39: K. 7 (10) M, *k. 2 C, (k. 1 M, p. 1 M) 5 times, C4F C, (k. 1 M, p. 1 M) 5

times, k. 2 C *, k. 10 M, rep. from * to *, k. 7 (10) M.

Row 41: K. 7 (10) M, * F.Cr., (k. 1 M, p. 1 M) 4 times, B.Cr., F.Cr., (k. 1 M, p. 1 M) 4 times, B.Cr. *, k. 10 M, rep. from * to *, k. 7 (10) M.

Row 43: K. 8 (11) M, * F.Cr., (k. 1 M, p. 1 M) 3 times, B.Cr., k. 2 M, F.Cr., (k. 1 M, p. 1 M) 3 times, B.Cr. *, k. 12 M, rep. from * to *, k. 8 (11) M.

Row 45: K. 9 (12) M, * F.Cr., (k. 1 M, p. 1 M) twice, B.Cr., k. 4 M, F.Cr., (k. 1 M, p. 1 M) twice, B.Cr. *, k. 14 M, rep. from * to *, k. 9 (12) M.

Row 47: K. 10 (13) M, * F.Cr., (k. 1 M, p. 1 M, B.Cr., k. 6 M, F.Cr., k. 1 M, p. 1 M, B.Cr. *, k. 16 M, rep. from * to *, k. 10 (13) M.

Row 49: K. 11 (14) M, * F.Cr., B.Cr., k. 8 M, F.Cr., B.Cr. *, k. 18 M, rep. from * to *, k. 11 (14) M.

Row 50: Work as for row 28.
(The Aran diamond and moss st. patt. is now complete.)

Rows 51–52: C.
Rows 53–58: M.
Rows 59–76: Joining in C, work in st. st. across *chart B*, working between appropriate lines for size required.
Rows 77–82: M.
Rows 83–88: Joining in C, and work in st. st., across *chart A*, working between appropriate lines for size required.
Rows 89–100: M.

To shape shoulders *Rows 101–106:* With M, cast off 8 sts. at beg. of next 4 rows, and 9 (10) sts. at beg. of foll. 2 rows.
Cast off rem. 30 (34) sts. for back neck.

Pocket linings (make 2)
Cast on 22 sts. using 7 mm. needles and M. Work 18 rows in st. st. beg. with a k. row. Leave sts. on a spare needle.

Right front
Cast on 40 sts. using 6 mm. needles and

M. Work 11 rows in k. 2, p. 2 rib, inc. 3 sts. across last row on *2nd size only* – 40 (43) sts.
Change to 7 mm. needles and work patt. as folls:
Rows 1–10: M.
Rows 11–16: Joining in C, work in st. st. across *chart A*, working from centre stitch across appropriate sts.
Rows 17–18: M.**

To place pocket lining *Row 19 (RS facing):* With M, k. 12 sts., slip next 22 sts. on to a stitch holder, and in place of these k. 22 sts. of 1st pocket lining, k. to end – 40 (43) sts.
Row 20: With M, p. across row.
Rows 21–24: With M, work in st. st. beg. with a k. row.
Rows 25–26: C.
Rows 27–50: Join in M and work Aran diamond and moss st. patt. as set for back (rows 27–50), placing patt. sts. of first row as folls:

Chart A

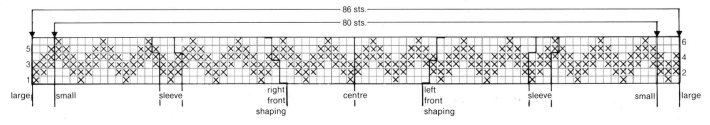

Chart B

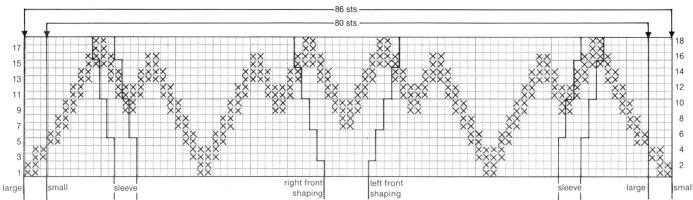

KEY   □ main shade   ✗ contrast

K. 10 M, C4F C, k. 10 M, C4F C, k. 12 (15) M.

Cont. in patt. as set for back until row 50 has been worked, *at the same time*, beg. at row 49, *shape neck* as folls:

Keeping patt. correct, dec. 1 st. at neck edge on next row and every foll. 4th row until 32 (35) sts. rem., then every foll. 3rd row until 25 (26) sts. rem.

Cont. in patt. keeping neck shaping as set.

Rows 51–52: C.
Rows 53–58: M.
Rows 59–76: Joining in C, work in st. st. across *chart B*, starting from appropriate position.
Rows 77–82: M.
Rows 83–88: Joining in C, work in st. st. across *chart A*, starting from appropriate position, and when 25 (26) sts. remain on needle, keep neck edge straight.
Rows 89–101: M.

To shape shoulder *Rows 102–104:* With M, cast off 8 sts. at beg. of next row and foll. alt. row.
Row 105: With M, k. across row.
Cast off rem. 9 (10) sts.

Left front
Cast on 40 sts. using 6 mm. needles and M. Now work as given for right front to **.

To place pocket lining *Row 19 (RS facing):* With M, k. 6 (9) sts., slip next 22 sts. on to a stitch holder and in place of these k. 22 sts. of 2nd pocket lining, k. to end – 40 (43) sts.
Cont. to work in patt. as given for right front, reversing all shapings and placing Aran diamond and moss st. patt. as folls and reading charts from appropriate positions:
Row 27: K. 12 (15) M, C4F C, k. 10 M, C4F C. k. 10 M.

Sleeves (make 2)
Cast on 30 (34) sts. using 6 mm. needles and M and work in double rib as follows:
Row 1 (RS facing): K. 2, * p. 2, k. 2, rep. from * to end.
Row 2: P. 2, * k. 2, p. 2, rep. from * to end.
Work in rib as set until 11 rib rows have been worked in all.

Inc. row: Rib 4 sts. (make 1 st. by picking up horizontal loop before next st. and k. into back of it, rib 2 sts.) 11 (13) times, make 1 st., rib 4 sts – 42 (48) sts.
Change to 7 mm. needles and work Aran and fair isle patts. as described below, and *at the same time* shape sleeve by inc. 1 st. at each end of every foll. 5th row until there are 64 (70) sts. on the needle, taking extra sts. into the patt. as they occur.
Rows 1–10: M.
Rows 11–16: Joining in C, work in st. st. across *chart A*, working between appropriate lines.
Rows 17–22: M.
Rows 23–34: Rep. rows 11–22 once more, taking care to keep patt. in line.
Rows 35–52: Joining in C, work in st. st. across *chart B*, working between appropriate lines. When 64 (70) sts. are on the needle, then work straight in patt.
Rows 53–62: M.
Cast off loosely and evenly.

TO MAKE UP AND BORDERS

Press all pieces gently on WS using a warm iron over a damp cloth. Join both shoulder seams using backstitch.

Front band Cast on 12 sts. using 6 mm. needles and M. Work 6 rows in k. 2, p. 2 rib.
Buttonhole row: Rib 5 sts., cast off 2 sts., rib to end.
Next row: Rib 5 sts., cast on 2 sts., rib to end. Work 14 rows in k. 2, p. 2 rib.
Rep. last 16 rows twice more, then first 2 rows once more (4 buttonholes worked).
Cont. straight in rib until band, when slightly stretched, fits up right front edge, across back neck and down left front edge. Cast off in rib.

Pocket edgings (alike) With 6 mm. needles, slip sts. from stitch holder on to left hand needle and work in rib as folls.:
Row 1: P. 2, * k. 2, p. 2 rep. from * to end.
Row 2: K. 2, * p. 2, k. 2 rep. from * to end.

Rep. rows 1 and 2 twice more. Cast off evenly in rib. Set in sleeves using a backstitch seam, matching centre of cast-off edges of sleeves to shoulder seams and allowing an armhole depth of approx. 25 (26) cm. (9¾ (10¼) in.). Backstitch side and sleeve seams. Sew on front band. Sew on buttons. Stitch pocket linings in position on WS, and pocket tops on RS. Press seams.

Moss Rose

The ridge pattern gives a touch of texture to this ultra plain jumper in mossy yarn with a roll collar.
Very easy.

MATERIALS

12 (13, 13) 50 g. balls Pingouin Givre, or 10 (11, 11) 50 g. balls Pingouin Vrille; a pair each 5 mm. (no. 6) and 5½ mm. (no. 5) knitting needles.

TENSION

17 stitches and 20 rows to 10 cm. (4 in.) using 5½ mm. (no. 5) needles and pattern.

MEASUREMENTS

To fit bust 86 (91, 97) cm., 34 (36, 38) in. Length 57 (58, 59) cm., 22½ (22¾, 23¼) in. Sleeve seam (all sizes) 48 cm., 19 in.

ABBREVIATIONS

beg., beginning; cont., continue; dec., decrease; foll., following; inc., increase; k., knit; p., purl; patt., pattern; rem., remaining; st(s)., stitch(es); st. st., stocking stitch.

INSTRUCTIONS

Back

With 5 mm. needles, cast on 81 (87, 93) sts. Work in k. 1, p. 1 rib for 7 cm. (3 in.), working an inc. at each end of last rib row – 83 (89, 95) sts. Change to 5½

mm. needles and patt. Work 6 rows in st. st., then purl the next 4 rows. These 10 rows form the patt. Cont. in patt. until work measures 35 cm. (13¾ in.) from beg.

To shape armholes Cast off 8 sts. at beg. of next 2 rows – 67 (73, 79) sts. ** Cont. straight in patt. until work measures 22 (23, 24) cm. (8¾ (9, 9½) in.) from armhole shaping.

To shape shoulders Cast off 8 sts. at beg. of next 4 rows. Leave rem. 35 (41, 47) sts. on a holder.

Front

Work as Back to **. Cont. straight in patt. until work measures 15 (16, 16) cm. (6 (6¼, 6¼) in.) from armhole shaping.

To shape neck *Next row:* Work 24 (27, 30), slip next 19 sts. on to a spare needle, work to end. Cont. on first group of sts. Dec. 1 st. at neck edge on every row until 16 sts. rem. Cont. on these sts. until front measures same as back to shoulder shaping, ending at side edge. Cast off 8 sts. at beg. of next row. Work 1 row. Cast off. Rejoin yarn at

neck edge to rem. group of sts. and complete to match first side.

Sleeves

With 5 mm. needles, cast on 39 (43, 47) sts., and work in k. 1, p. 1 rib for 7 cm. (2¼ in.).
Inc. row: Rib 1 (3, 1), * inc. in next st., rib 3 (3, 4); rep. from * to last 2 (4, 1) sts., inc. in next st., rib 1 (3, 0). Change to 6 mm. needles and work in patt. as on back, inc. 1 st. at each end of every foll. 6th row until there are 75 (79, 83) sts. Cont. on these sts. until sleeve seam measures 48 cm. (19 in.) from beg. Cast off.

Collar

Join right shoulder seam. Using 5 mm. needles, with right side facing, pick up and k. 18 sts. along left front neck, k. across 19 sts. from front neck, pick up and k. 18 sts. along right front neck, and k. across 35 sts. from back – 90 sts. Now work 4 patt. repeats but at end of 4th patt. work only 3 purl rows. Cast off purlwise.

TO MAKE UP

Join left shoulder and collar seam. Set in sleeves, so that cast off edges of sleeves are sewn to straight edges of armholes and cast off groups of 8 sts. are joined to top edges of sleeve seam. Join side and sleeve seams.

Le Rouge and le Noir

MATERIALS

10 (11) 50 g. balls Pingouin Typhon in main shade (black); 8 (9) 50 g. balls Pingouin Typhon in contrast shade (red); a pair each 5½ mm. (no. 5) and 6½ mm. (no. 3) knitting needles.

TENSION

14 stitches and 16 rows to 10 cm. (4 in.) over fair isle using 6½ mm.needles.

MEASUREMENTS

To fit bust 81–86 (91–97) cm., 32–34 (36–38) in. (loosely).
Length 52 (58) cm., 20½ (23) in.
Sleeve seam (all sizes) 48 cm., 19 in.

ABBREVIATIONS

beg., beginning; CS, contrast shade, red; inc., increase; k., knit; MS, main shade, black; p., purl; patt., pattern; rem., remaining; st(s)., stitch(es); st. st., stocking stitch.

INSTRUCTIONS

Back
With 5½ mm. needles and MS, cast on 77 (87) sts. Work in k. 1, p. 1 rib for 7 rows. Change to 6½ mm. needles. Work in st. st. for 2 rows. Now work fair isle patt. from chart, working rows 1 to 30 twice. ** Now work fair isle until length measures 52 (53) cm. (20½ (21) in.) from beg.

To shape shoulders Cast off 25 (29) sts. at beg. of next 2 rows. Leave rem. 27 (29) sts. on a spare needle.

Front
Exactly as back to **. Now work fair isle until length measures 47 (48) cm. (18½ (19) in.) from beg.

To shape neck Work 31 (36) turn; work on these sts. only. Dec. 1 st. at neck edge on every row to 25 (29) sts. When length

matches back, cast off. Slip the centre 15 sts. on to a spare needle. Rejoin yarn and complete other side of neck to match.

Sleeves
With 5½ mm. needles, and MS, cast on 31 (35) sts. Work in k. 1, p. 1 rib for 11 rows, working 6 incs. evenly along last rib row – 37 (41) sts. Change to 6½ mm. needles. Now work fair isle patt. from chart, beg. where indicated on chart, and at the same time, inc. 1 st. at each end of every foll. 4th row, working extra sts. into patt. to 67 (71) sts. Cast off loosely.

Collar
Join right shoulder seam. With 6 mm. needles, using black yarn with right side facing, pick up and k. 9 sts. along left front neck, k. across the 15 sts. of front neck, pick up and k. 9 st. along right front neck, then k. across the 27 (29) sts. of back neck. Beg. p. row, work in st. st. until collar measures 12 cm. (4¾ in.) from beg. Cast off loosely.

TO MAKE UP

Press on reverse side (except rib) with a warm iron and a damp cloth. Join left shoulder seam. Join collar seam on the k. side of collar. Sew on sleeves. Join sleeve seams and side seams. Press all seams.

> Although the sweater pattern is complicated, you are only using two colours so it is easier to concentrate on each row. A lovely thick yarn speeds the work along. You may prefer to knit the skirt to a more classic length if you daren't risk the mini length.

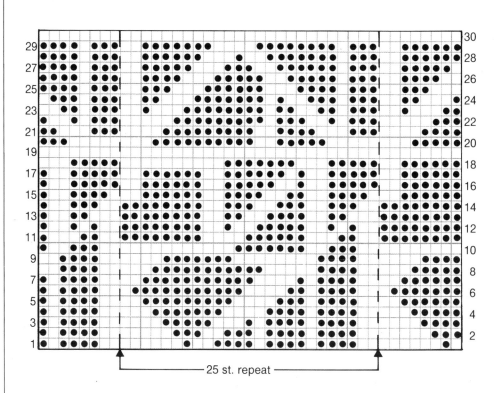

25 st. repeat

KEY ☐ main shade (black) ● contrast (red)

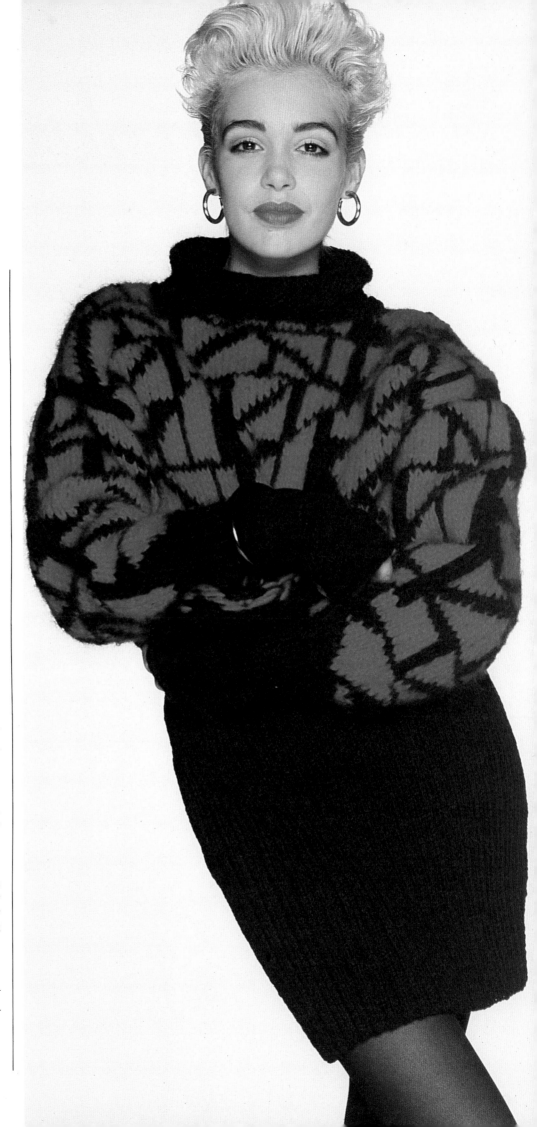

TUBE SKIRT

MATERIALS

7 (8) 50 g. balls Pingouin Pingofrance (black); a pair 5 mm. (no. 6) knitting needles.

TENSION

13 sts. and 13 rows to 5 cm. (2 in.) over k. 2 p. 2 rib using yarn double.

MEASUREMENTS

To fit hip size 81–86 (91–97) cm., 32–34 (36–38) in.
Length 48 cm., 19 in.

ABBREVIATIONS

cont., continue; dec., decrease; foll., following; inc., increase; k., knit; p., purl; patt., pattern; rem., remain; rep., repeat; st(s)., stitch(es).

INSTRUCTIONS

Note Yarn is used double throughout.

Back and front (both alike)
With 5 mm. needles, using yarn double throughout, cast on 110 (118) sts. Now work the foll. patt.:
Row 1: K. 2 (p. 2, k. 2) to end.
Row 2: P. 2 (k. 2, p. 2) to end.
These 2 rows form patt. Work the 2 rows 45 (49) times in all – 90 (98) rows. Now dec. 1 st. at each end of next and every foll. 4th row until 98 (106) sts. rem. Work patt. twice (3 times) more. Work row 1 once more. Cast off ribwise.

TO MAKE UP

Join side seams.

Sapphire

MATERIALS

10 (11, 11) 50 g. balls Pingouin Ruban; a pair each 7½ mm. (no. 1) and 6½ mm. (no. 3) knitting needles; a 6½ mm. (no. 3) circular knitting needle, 60 cm.

Note Pingouin Ruban is available by mail order from Ries Wools, 243 High Holborn, London WC1V 7DZ.
Important: This yarn is circular knitted and pressed flat to give a smooth satin look. Because of the relatively heavy nature of the yarn, the garment will tend to drop in length when worn. For this reason it has additional width. Take all measurements with work hanging from needles. To prevent the yarn unravelling knot each cut end tightly. Fasten off all ends securely and don't sew seams too tightly.

TENSION

13 stitches and 17 rows to 10 cm. (4 in.) over stocking stitch using 7½ mm. (no. 1) needles.

MEASUREMENTS

To fit bust 86 (91, 97) cm., 34 (36, 38) in. Length from shoulder approx. 56 (57, 58) cm., 22 (22½, 22¾) in.

ABBREVIATIONS

alt., alternate; beg., beginning; cont., continue; dec., decrease; foll., following; inc., increase; k., knit; p., purl; patt., pattern; rem., remaining; rep., repeat; RS, right side; st(s)., stitch(es); st. st., stocking stitch; tog., together; WS, wrong side.

INSTRUCTIONS

Note This is worked in one piece.

Beg. at lower edge of front. With 6½ mm. needles, cast on 81 (85, 89) sts. Work 10 cm. in k. 1, p. 1 rib, beg. alt. rows p. 1. Change to 7½ mm. needles. Cont. in st. st. until front measures 47 (48, 49) cm. (18½ (19, 19¼) in.) from cast-on edge and ending with a p. row.

To shape neck Row 1: K. 29 (31, 33) sts., k. 2 tog., turn. Cont. on these sts. only for first side and leave rem. sts. on a spare needle. ** Dec. 1 st. at neck edge on the next 8 rows – 22 (24, 26) sts. Work 6 rows straight. Mark each end of last row to denote shoulder. Inc. 1 st. at neck edge on next 6 rows – 28 (30, 32) sts. **. Fasten off and leave sts. on a spare needle.
With RS of work facing, sl. centre 19 sts. on to a stitch holder, rejoin yarn to inner end of 1st set of sts., k. 2 tog., k. to end. Work as first side from ** to **.
Joining row: P. 28 (30, 32) sts., cast on 25 sts., p. across 28 (30, 32) sts. of first side – 81 (85, 89) sts.
Cont. straight until the same number of rows of st. st. have been worked as on front from top of rib to shoulder markers, ending with a p. row. Change to 6½ mm. needles. Work 10 cm. in k. 1, p. 1 rib, beg. alt. rows p. 1. Cast off in rib.

Neckband
With 6½ mm. circular needle, pick up and k. 43 sts. around back neck and 16 sts. down left front neck, k. across 19 sts. at centre front neck then pick up and k. 16 sts. up right front neck – 94 sts. Work 5 rounds in k. 1, p. 1 rib. Cast off in rib.

TO MAKE UP

Do not press. Join side seams to within 20 (21, 22) cm. (8 (8½, 8¾) in.) of shoulder markers. Remove markers.

Abstract

You'll find knitting this surprisingly quick, however large the size. Try primary colours or black, white or grey.

MATERIALS

13 (14) 50 g. balls Pingouin Iceberg Marine (A), 5 balls Londres (B) and 2 balls Grenat (C); two each 4½ mm. (no. 7) and 5½ mm. (no. 5) knitting needles.

TENSION

7 stitches and 10 rows to 5 cm. (2 in.) using 5½ mm. (no. 5) needles.

MEASUREMENTS

To fit chest 91–97 (102–107) cm., 36–38 (40–42) in.
Length 63 (65) cm., 24¾ (25½) in.
Sleeve seam with turned-back cuff (all sizes) 45 (46) cm., 17¾ (18) in.

ABBREVIATIONS

beg., beginning; dec., decrease; inc., increase; k., knit; p. purl; patt., pattern; rep., repeat; sts., stitches; st.st., stocking stitch; tog., together.

INSTRUCTIONS

Back

With 4½ mm. needles and A cast on 70 (76) sts. Work 14 rows k. 1, p. 1 rib. Change to 5½ mm. needles. Beg. k., continue in st.st., inc. 1 st. each end of next and every following 6th row until there are 76 (82) sts. Work 3 rows *.
Continue in block patt. thus:
Row 1: K. 33 (36) B, 1 C, 42 (45) A.
Row 2: P. 41 (44) A, 2 C, 33 (36) B.
Row 3: K. 33 (36) B, 3 C, 40 (43) A.
Row 4: P. 39 (42) A, 4 C, 33 (36) B.
Row 5: K. 33 (36) B, 5 C, 38 (41) A.
Row 6: P. 37 (40) A, 6 C, 33 (36) B.
Continue in this way working 1 st. more in C and 1 st. less in A on every following row until row reading: p. 5 (6) A, 38 (40) C, 33 (36) B has been worked.
Next row: K. 33 (36) A, 38 (40) C, 5 (6) A.
Next row: P. 5 (6) A, 38 (40) C, 33 (36) A.
Rep. last 2 rows 7 times more.

To shape armhole With patt. as set. cast off 3 (4) sts. at beg. of next 2 rows, then dec. 1 st. at beg. of following 4 rows – 66 (70) sts. Patt. 2 rows straight.
Next row: K. 28 (30) A, 38 (40) B.
Next row: P. 37 (39) B, 29 (31) A.
Next row: K. 30 (32) A, 36 (38) B.
Next row: P. 35 (37) B, 31 (33) A **.
Continue in this way working 1 st. more in A and 1 st. less in B on every following row until row reading: p. 9 B, 57 (61) A has been worked.

To shape neck Next row: K. 23 (24) A, cast off 20 (22) sts., k. 15 (16) A, 8 B. Continue on last set of sts. only. Still working patt. as set, dec. 1 st. at neck edge on next 2 rows. Patt. 2 rows straight.

To shape shoulders Cast off 11 sts. at beg. of next row. Work 1 row. Cast off. With wrong side facing, rejoin A to remaining sts. and using A only, work to match other side, reversing neck and shoulder shapings.

Front

As back to *. Continue in block patt. thus:
Row 1: K. 42 (45) A, 1 C, 33 (36) B.
Row 2: P. 33 (36) B, 2 C, 41 (44) A.
Row 3: K. 40 (43) A, 3 C, 33 (36) B.
Row 4: P. 33 (36) B, 4 C, 39 (42) A.
Reversing patt. by working rows in reverse in this way, continue as given for back to **. Continue straight, working 1 st. less in B and 1 st. more in A until row reading: P. 53 (57) A, 13 B has been worked.

To shape neck Next row: K. 12 B, 13 (14) A, turn. Continue on these sts. only. Still working patt. as set, dec. 1 st. at neck edge on next 4 rows. Patt 3 rows straight.

To shape shoulders Cast off 11 sts. at beg. of next row. Work 1 row. Cast off. With right side facing, rejoin A to inner end of remaining sts., cast off centre 16 (18) sts. and with A only work other side to match, reversing neck and shoulder shapings.

Sleeves

Right: With 4½ mm. needles and A cast on 32 (36) sts. Rib 14 cm. (5½ in.) as back. Change to 5½ mm. needles. With A continue in st. st., inc. 1 st. each end of 9th and every following 6th row until there are 38 (42) sts. P. 1 row. Break off A; join B. Continue inc. 1 st. each end of 5th and every following 6th row until 38 (40) rows B have been worked. Break off B; join A. Continue inc. as set until there are 54 (58) sts. Work 7 (9) rows straight. To shape top cast off 3 (4) sts. at beg. of next 2 rows *. Dec. 1 st. at beg. of every row until 32 sts. remain. Dec. 1 st. each end of following 8 rows. Cast off.
Left: Using A only, work as right to *. Dec. 1 st. at beg. of next 6 rows. Break off A; join B and complete as right.

Neckband

Join right shoulder seam. With right side facing, using 4½ mm. needles and A pick up and k. 36 (38) sts. evenly around front neck and 34 (36) sts. evenly around back neck. Rib 8 rows. Cast off ribwise.

TO MAKE UP

Press work. Join left shoulder and neckband seam. Set in sleeves. Join side and sleeve seams, reversing seam for turned-back cuff. Press seams.

Body Dressing

RIBBED POLO NECK SWEATER

MATERIALS

7 (7, 8) 50 g. balls Hayfield Grampian DK in black; a pair 4 mm. (no. 8) knitting needles; a 3¾ mm. (no. 9) circular needle; spare needles; stitch holder.

MEASUREMENTS

To fit bust 86 (91, 97) cm., 34 (36, 38) in.
Actual measurement 92 (99, 106) cm., 36 (39, 41¾) in.
Length from shoulder 54 (56, 58) cm., 21½ (22, 23) in.
Sleeve seam 46 cm., 18 in.

TENSION

25 stitches to 10.5 cm. (4 in.) over double rib when slightly stretched using 4 mm. (no. 8) needles.

ABBREVIATIONS

beg., beginning; cont., continue; dec., decrease; foll., following; inc., increase; k., knit; p., purl; patt., pattern; rem., remaining; rep., repeat; RS, right side; st(s)., stitch(es); WS, wrong side

INSTRUCTIONS

Note All casting off should be done ribwise.

Back

With 4 mm. needles, cast on 110 (118, 126) sts., and work in double rib as follows:
Row 1 (RS): K. 2, * p. 2, k. 2, rep. from * to end.
Row 2: P. 2, * k. 2, p. 2, rep. from * to end.
These 2 rows form the patt. and are repeated throughout. Cont. straight in patt. until back measures 36 (37, 38) cm. (14¼ (14½, 15) in.) from cast-on edge, ending with a WS row.

Fit and cling body conscious knits mean skinny ribby sweaters and tight ribby skirts, which are really easy to make.

To shape armholes Keeping rib correct, cast off 8 sts. at beg. of next 4 rows (78 (86, 94) sts.) **. Cont. straight in patt. until back measures 18 (19, 20) cm. (7 (7½, 8) in.) from beg. of armhole shaping, ending with a WS row.

To slope shoulders Cast off 8 sts. at beg. of next 2 rows, then 7 (9, 11) sts. at beg. of foll. 2 rows. Leave rem. 48 (52, 56) sts. on a spare needle for back neck.

Front

Work exactly as for back to **. Cont. straight in patt. until front measures 11 (12, 13) cm. (4¼ (4¾, 5) in.) from beg. of armhole shaping, ending with a WS row.

To shape front neck Next row: Rib 25 (29, 33), work 2 tog., turn and work on these sts. only for first side. Leave rem. sts. on a spare needle.
*** Dec. 1 st. at neck edge on every row until 15 (17, 19) sts. rem. Cont. straight in patt. until front measures the same as back to shoulder shaping, ending at armhole edge.

To slope shoulders Cast off 8 sts. at beg. of next row. Work 1 row then cast off rem. 7 (9, 11) sts. With RS facing, slip centre 24 sts. on to a stitch holder, rejoin yarn, work 2 tog., rib to end – 26 (30, 34) sts. Complete to match first side, working from *** to end.

Sleeves (make 2)

Using 4 mm. needles, cast on 46 (50, 54) sts. and work 6 cm. in double rib as for back. Working the increased sts. into the rib as they occur, inc. 1 st. at both ends of next row and every foll. 4th row until there are 94 (98, 102) sts. on the needle. Cont. straight in patt. until sleeve measures 46 cm. (18¼ in.) (or length required) from cast-on edge, ending with a

---

WS row. Place a marker at both ends of last row. Work a further 6 cm. (2½ in.) in rib. Cast off in rib.

Collar

Join shoulder seams. With RS facing, and using 3¾ mm. circular needle, pick up and k. 18 sts. from row ends of left front neck, k. across the 24 sts. of centre front neck, pick up and k. 18 sts. from row ends of right front neck, then k. across the 48 (52, 56) sts. of back neck – 108 (112, 116) sts. Work 14 cm. (5½ in.) *in rounds* of k. 2 p. 2 rib. Cast off in rib.

TO MAKE UP

Set in sleeves, sewing the row ends above markers to the sts. cast off for armholes on both back and front and cast-off edge of sleeves to the straight row ends of armholes. Join side seams and sleeve seams.

MINI SKIRT

MATERIALS

6 (7) 50 g. balls Hayfield Grampian DK in black (used double); a pair 4 mm. (no. 8) knitting needles.

TENSION

24 stitches to 10.5 cm. (4¼ in.) over flat rib, with yarn used double using 4 mm. needles.

MEASUREMENTS

To fit sizes 10–12 and 12–14.
Length: 43 (45) cm., 17 (17¾) in.

ABBREVIATIONS

As for sweater.

Ninotchka

INSTRUCTIONS

Note Yarn is used double throughout.

Back and front (both alike)
With 4 mm. needles, and yarn used double, cast on 92 (102) sts. and work in flat rib as follows:
Row 1 (RS): P. 2, * k. 3, p. 2, rep. from * to end.
Row 2: K. 2, * p. 3, k. 2, rep. from * to end.
These 2 rows form the patt. and are repeated throughout. Cont. straight in patt. until work measures 32 (34) cm. (12½ (13¼) in.) from cast-on edge. Keeping rib correct, dec. 1 st. at both ends of next row and every foll. 4th row until 82 (92) sts. remain. Cont. straight in rib until work measures 43 (45) cm. (16½ (17¾) in.) from cast-on edge. Cast off in rib.

TO MAKE UP

Join side seams. Lightly press seams.

LEGGINGS

MATERIALS

3 50 g. balls Hayfield Grampian DK in black; a pair 4 mm. (no. 8) knitting needles.

MEASUREMENTS

Length 62.5 cm., 24½ in.

ABBREVIATIONS AND TENSION

As for sweater.

INSTRUCTIONS

With 4 mm. needles, cast on 62 sts. and work in double rib as for sweater.
Rep. the 2 rows of rib until work measures 16 cm. (6¼ in.) from cast-on edge. Keeping rib correct, inc. 1 st. at both ends of next row and every foll. 3rd row until 78 sts. are on the needle. Cont. straight in rib until work measures 42 cm. (16½ in.) from cast-on edge. Now inc. 1 st. at both ends of next row and every foll. 4th row until 94 sts. are on the needle. Cont. straight in rib until work measures 62.5 cm. (24½ in.) from cast-on edge (or required length). Cast off in rib.

TO MAKE UP

Join seam. Lightly press seam.

Ninotchka

MATERIALS

8 (9) 50 g. balls Pingouin Coton Naturel 8 Fils, 4 (5) 50 g. balls Pingouin Mohair 50, 10 (11) 50 g. balls Sport Laine, 3 (3) 50 g. balls Pingouin Orage, 3 (4) 50 g. balls Pingouin Bourrette de Soie, Pingouin Fourrure optional (we used 2 m.); a pair each 8 mm. (no. 0) and 10 mm. (no. 000) knitting needles; a cable needle.

TENSION

9 stitches and 15 rows to 10 cm. (4 in.) over moss stitch using 10 mm. (no. 000) needles and 3 strands of yarn (see *Note* below).

MEASUREMENTS

To fit bust 81–86 (91–97) cm., 32–34 (36–38) in. loosely.
Length 78 cm., 30¾ in.
Sleeve seam, including insert (both sizes), 48 cm., 19 in.

ABBREVIATIONS

A, Coton Naturel; B, Mohair 50; C, Sport Laine; D, Orage; E, Bourrette de Soie; cable 6, sl. next 3 sts. on to cable needle to front of work, k. 3, then k. 3 from cable needle; cable 10, sl. next 5 sts. on to cable to front of work, k. 5, then k. 5 from cable needle (figures in square brackets are worked the number of times stated); g. st., garter stitch; inc., increase; k., knit; m. st., moss stitch; p., purl; sl., slip; st(s)., stitch(es).

INSTRUCTIONS

Note For main part one strand each of A, B and C are used together and will be referred to as ABC; for cables and garter stitch inserts one strand each of D and E are used together and will be referred to as DE.

If you love mixing different yarns and textures try this pattern which combines cotton, mohair and wool as well as a variety of different stitches. Take extra care with the sewing up to see that all your seams match.

Front
Using 8 mm. needles and ABC cast on 65 (73) sts.
Row 1: K. 1 [p. 1, k. 1] to end.
Row 2: P. 1 [k. 1, p. 1] to end.
Repeat these 2 rows 3 times more, inc. one st. in centre of last row – 66 (74) sts. Change to 10 mm. needles.
** *Row 1:* K. 2 [p. 2, k. 2] 6 (7) times, turn and leave remaining sts. on a spare needle. Continue on these 26 (30) sts. for left front.
Row 2: P. 2 [k. 2, p. 2] to end.
Row 3: As row 2.
Row 4: As row 1.
These 4 rows form the pattern for double moss st.; repeat them 14 times more.
Next row: pattern 8 (10), turn and leave remaining sts. on a spare needle. Continue on these 8 (10) sts., work 25 more rows. Break off yarn and leave sts. on a holder. Return to the 18 (20) sts. on spare needle, with right side facing sl. the first 10 sts. on to a holder, rejoin ABC and pattern to end. Continue on these sts., work 25 more rows. Break off yarn and leave sts. on a holder. Return to the 10 sts. on holder: with right side facing join in DE.
Row 1: P. 2, k. 6, p. 2.
Row 2: K. 2, p. 6, k. 2.
Repeat these 2 rows twice more.
Row 7: P. 2, cable 6, p. 2.
Row 8: As row 2.
Rows 9 to 12: Repeat rows 1 and 2 twice.
Repeat these 12 rows once more. Break off yarn. With DE and right side facing, k. the first 8 (10) sts. which were left, k. the 10 sts. of cable panel, then k. the remaining 8 (10) sts. Work 9 rows in g. st. Break off DE, rejoin ABC and work 12 rows in pattern as at beginning. Cast off. Return to the sts. on spare needle; using

10 mm. needles and DE and with right side facing p. 2, k. 10, p. 2, turn and continue on these sts. for centre front panel.
Row 2: K. 2, p. 10, k. 2.
Repeat these 2 rows twice more.
Row 7: P. 2, cable 10, p. 2.
Row 8: As row 2.
Rows 9 to 12: Repeat rows 1 and 2 twice more. Repeat these 12 rows until work measures the same as left front panel ending with a wrong side row. Cast off. Return to the remaining 26 (30) sts. on spare needle and work right front panel; using 10 mm. needles and ABC [k. 1, p. 1] to end. Repeat this row (m. st.) 35 times more.
Change to DE and work 10 rows in g. st. Change to ABC and continue in m. st. as before, work 38 rows.
Next row: m. st. 8 (10), turn and leave remaining sts. on a spare needle. Continue on these sts., work 25 rows. Cast off. Return to the sts. on spare needle, with right side facing join in DE, p. 2, k. 6, p. 2, turn and leave remaining sts. on the spare needle. Continue on these sts., work as for cable panel on left front. Cast off.
Return to the remaining 8 (10) sts. on spare needle, rejoin ABC and m. st. to end. Work 25 more rows. Cast off. Join seams. Place markers on shoulders about 20 (23) cm. (8(9¼) in.) from each side.

Back
Work as given for front to **.
Next row: [K. 1, p. 1] 13 (15) times, turn and continue on these 26 (30) sts. for right back panel, work as given for right front panel. Return to the sts. on spare needle, join in DE and work centre panel on next 14 sts. as given for front. Return to the remaining 26 (30) sts. on spare needle, rejoin ABC and work as given for left front panel. Join seams and place markers for shoulders as on front.

Neckband
Join right shoulder seam.
Using 8 mm. needles and ABC and with right side facing pick up and k. 57 (61) sts. round neck. Beginning with a 2nd row, work 5 rows in rib as on front. Cast off in rib.

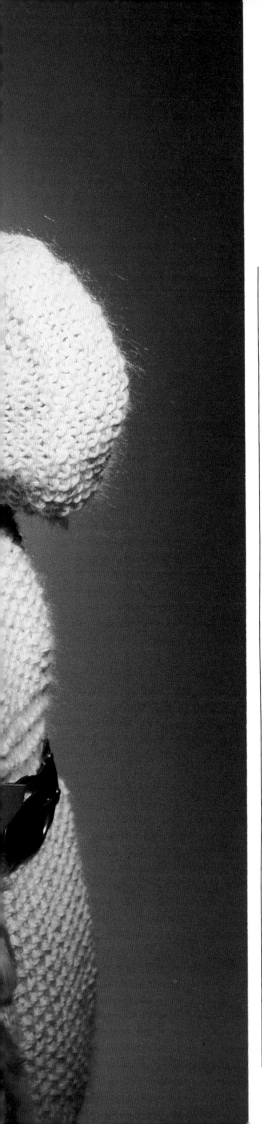

Left sleeve

Using 8 mm. needles and ABC cast on 27 (31) sts. and work 12 rows in rib as on front, inc. one st. in centre of last row – 28 (32) sts. Change to 10 mm. needles. **

Next row: K. 0 (1), p. 1 (2), [k. 2, p. 2] twice, turn and leave remaining sts. on a spare needle.

Continue on these 9 (11) sts. in double m. st., inc. one st. at beginning (outer edge) of 5th and every following 4th row until there are 19 (21) sts., then continue without shaping until 48 rows have been worked in pattern. Cast off. Return to the sts. on spare needle; with right side facing slip first 10 sts. on to a holder, rejoin ABC [p. 2, k. 2] twice, p. 1 (2), k. 0 (1). Continue to match first side, reversing shaping by inc. at end of 5th and every following 4th row. Return to the 10 sts. on holder, using 10 mm. needles and DE and with right side facing p. 2, k. 6, p. 2. Continue on these sts. as for panel on left front until work measures the same as side pieces, ending with a wrong side row. Cast off.

Right sleeve

Work as given for left sleeve to **.

Next row: [k. 1, p. 1] to end.

Continue in m. st. across all sts. inc. one st. at each end of 5th and every following 4th row until there are 36 (40) sts., then work 1 row. Break off ABC, join in DE and work 10 rows in g. st., inc. at each end of 3rd and 7th rows. Break off DE, rejoin ABC and continue in m. st., inc. at each end of next and every following 4th row until there are 46 (50) sts., then continue without shaping until 20 rows have been worked. Cast off.

Sleeve inserts (make 2)

Using 10 mm. needles and DE cast on 14 sts. and work as for centre front panel until insert fits across top of sleeve. Cast off.

TO MAKE UP

Do not press. Join left shoulder seam and neckband. Sew inserts across top of sleeves, then sew in sleeves, placing centre of sleeves to shoulder seams. Join side and sleeve seams. Weave strips of fur through cables (optional).

Useful Addresses

Write to the addresses below for the head office or agent of the yarn spinner for stockist information. Where there is no agent the addresses of main stockists are given. Where the yarn is available only by mail order, this address is given.

ALAFOSS LOPI
UK
Scotnord Ltd.
P.O. Box 27
Athey Street
Macclesfield
Cheshire SK11 8EA
UK

Mail order
The Yarn Store
8 Ganton Street
London W1
UK

Colourspun
18a Camden Road
Camden Town
London NW1 94A
UK

USA distributor
Reynolds Yarns Inc.
15 Oser Avenue
Hauppauge
New York 11788
USA

Canada distributor
R. Stein Yarn Corp.
Place de la Mode
5800 St. Denis Street
Suite 303
Montreal
Quebec H2S 3L5
Canada

Australia distributor
Scandic Import Co.
P.O. Box 120
Vermont
Victoria 3133
Australia

HAYFIELD
UK
Hayfield Textiles Ltd.
Hayfield Mills
Glusburn
Nr. Keighley
W. Yorks BD20 8QP
UK

USA wholesaler
Shepherd Wools Inc.
923 Industry Drive
Seattle
Washington 98188
USA

Canada wholesaler
Craftsmen Distributors Inc.
4166 Halifax Street
Burnaby
British Columbia
Canada

Australia agent
E. C. Birch Pty. Ltd.
153 Bridge Road
Richmond 3121
Victoria
Australia

Australia wholesaler
Panda Yarns International Pty. Ltd.
17–27 Brunswick Road
East Brunswick
Victoria 3057
Australia

S. Africa agent
A & H Agencies
392 Commissioners Street
Fair View
Johannesburg 2094
S. Africa

LAINES ANNY BLATT
UK mail order
Ries Wools
243 High Holborn
London WC1V 7DZ
UK

USA agent
Irma Marcos
29775 North Western Highway
Southfield
Michigan 48034
USA

Canada agent
Diamond Yarn (Canada) Corp.
9697 St. Lawrence Blvd.
Montreal
Quebec
Canada H3L 2N1

MAXWELL CARTLIDGE
UK mail order
P.O. Box 33
Colchester
Essex
UK

PATONS and JAEGER
UK
Jaeger Handknitting *or*
Patons & Baldwins Ltd.
Alloa
Clackmannanshire
Scotland
UK

Mail order
Woolfayre Ltd.
120 High Street
Northallerton
W. Yorks.
UK

USA
C. J. Bates and Sons Ltd.
Route 9a
Chester
Connecticut 06412
USA

Canada agent
Patons & Baldwins (Canada) Ltd.
1001 Roselawn Avenue
Toronto
Canada

Australia agent
Coats & Patons Aust. Ltd.
321–355 Fern Tree Gully Road
P.O. Box 110
Mount Waverley
Victoria 3149
Australia

S. Africa
Mr Bob Theis
Marketing Manager
Patons & Baldwins (S. Africa) Pty. Ltd.
P.O. Box 33
Randfontein 1760
S. Africa

PINGOUIN
UK
French Wools Ltd.
7–11 Lexington Street
London W1R 4BU
UK

Head office and mail order
Mr R. Mesdagh
BP 9110
59061 Roubaix
Cedex 1
France

USA agent
Pingouin-Promafil Corp. (USA)
P.O. Box 100
Highway 45
Jamestown
S. Carolina 29453 USA

Useful Addresses

Canada agent
Promafil (Canada) Ltd.
1500 Rue Jules Poitras
379 St Laurent
Quebec H4N 1X7
Canada

Australia stockist
The Needlewoman
308 Centrepoint
Murray Street
Hobart
Tasmania 7000

S. Africa agent
Romatex/Yarns and Wools
P.O. Box 12
Jacobs 4026
Natal
S. Africa

ROWAN
UK
Rowan Yarns
Green Lane Mill
Holmfirth
W. Yorkshire HD7 1RW
UK

USA
Westminster Trading
5 Northern Blvd
Amhurst
New Hampshire 03031
USA

Canada
Estelle
38 Continental Place
Scarborough
Ontario M1R 2TH
Canada

Australia
Sunspun
195 Canterbury Road
Canterbury 3126
Australia

New Zealand
Creative Fashion Centre
P.O. Box 45083
Epuni Railway
Lower Hutt
New Zealand

South Africa
Jumpers
Shop 17
Admiral's Court
31 Tyrwhitt Avenue
Rosebank 2196
Johannesburg
S. Africa

SIRDAR
UK
Sirdar PLC
Flanshaw Lane
Alverthorpe
Wakefield
W. Yorkshire WS2 9ND
UK

USA distributor
Kendex Corp.
P.O. Box 1909
Moorpark
California 93020
USA

Canada distributors
Diamond Yarn (Canada) Corp.
153 Bridgeland Ave
Unit 11
Toronto
Ontario M6A 2Y6
Canada

Diamond Yarn (Canada) Corp.
9697 St. Lawrence Blvd.
Montreal
Quebec H3L 2N1
Canada

Australia distributor
Sirdar (Australia) Pty Ltd.
P.O. Box 110
Mount Waverley
Victoria 3149
Australia

New Zealand distributor
Alltex International
106 Parnell Road
P.O. Box 2500
Auckland
New Zealand

South Africa distributor
Patons and Baldwins
P.O. Box 33
Randfontein 1760
South Africa

SUNBEAM
UK
Richard Ingram & Co. Ltd
Crawshaw Mills
Pudsey
Leeds LS28 7BS
W. Yorkshire
UK

TWILLEYS
UK
H. G. Twilley Ltd.
Roman Mill
Stamford
Lincs. PE9 1BG
UK

USA agent
House of Settler
2120 Broadway
Luvvock
Texas
USA

Canada agent
S. R. Kertzer Ltd.
257 Adelaide Street W.
Toronto N5H MI
Ontario
Canada

Australia agent
Panda Yarns International Pty Ltd.
17–27 Brunswick Road
East Brunswick 3057
Victoria
Australia

S. Africa agents
S. W. Nyman Ltd.
P.O. Box 292
Durban 4000
S. Africa

Chester Mortonson Ltd.
P.O. Box 11179
Johannesburg 2000
S. Africa